Astronomy
and the Bible

Astronomy
and the Bible

Questions and Answers
Second Edition

Donald B. DeYoung

Foreword by John C. Whitcomb

A Division of Baker Book House Co
Grand Rapids, Michigan 49516

Published by Baker Books
a division of Baker Book House Company
P.O. Box 6287, Grand Rapids, MI 49516-6287

Printed in the United States of America

Library of Congress Cataloging-in-Publication Data

DeYoung, Donald B.
    Astronomy and the Bible : questions and answers / Donald B. DeYoung ; foreword by John C. Whitcomb.—2nd ed.
        p.   cm.
    Includes bibliographical references and index.
    ISBN 0-8010-6225-X (paper)
    1. Astronomy in the Bible—Miscellanea. 2. Astronomy—Miscellanea. I. Title.
    BS655.D44 2000
    220.8'52—dc21   99-054289

For current information about all releases from Baker Book House, visit our web site:

http://www.bakerbooks.com

Dedication

This book is dedicated to my mother, Florence, and in memory of my dad, John. They first introduced me to God's creation: planting seeds and picking blueberries, watching lightning and counting stars. Their faithful Christian lives have been the kind of example so desperately needed today.

Contents

Part 2 The Solar System

Part 3 The Stars

Part 4 Galaxies and the Universe

Part 5 General Science

Part 6 Technical Terms and Ideas

Part 7 Additional Astronomy Questions

Foreword

Nearly 3,000 years separate David, shepherd boy and amateur astronomer of Bethlehem-Judah, and Donald DeYoung, professor and physicist from Winona Lake, Indiana. What David knew about the magnitude and functions of the universe was almost nothing compared to the information available today. David lived in the "prescientific age" and thus was aware of only the sun, the earth's moon, four or five moving planets, and about 3,000 fixed stars beyond. By contrast, as beneficiaries of late-twentieth-century scientific technology, Donald DeYoung and his contemporaries know vastly more about the physical properties and functions of the sun, the moon, eight other planets, more than 50 moons, thousands of asteroids and comets, electromagnetic radiation, gravitational and other force fields, 100 billion stars in our Milky Way Galaxy, and billions of galaxies beyond.

David may not have been technically knowledgeable about astronomy, but he was a wholehearted *believer* in his Creator and Lord. He was also a man after God's own heart (Acts 13:22). Even as a young lad, tending his father's flocks by night, David could intuitively relate what he saw in the sky above him to God's written revelation in Genesis 1. He wrote in Psalm 8:3–4:

When I consider your heavens,
  the work of your fingers,
the moon and the stars,
  which you have set in place,
what is man that you are mindful of him?

He was totally committed to the proposition that God was the great Designer and Creator of the universe.

Tragically, in our great "space age," there are very few professional scientists with full academic credentials who share David's faith. One of these is Donald B. DeYoung, my friend and colleague of nearly twenty years at Grace Schools, Winona Lake, Indiana. In his numerous courses, seminars, and publications on astronomy, he has clearly demonstrated that he knows and loves the God of creation, and takes the Genesis record with utmost seriousness. More consistently than most Christian astrophysicists, he interprets empirical astronomic data within the framework of God's special revelation in Scripture. Since God's Word is here given the preeminence, the reader may have confidence that the answers provided are not merely the whims of human speculation.

It brings me great joy, therefore, to commend this fascinating book to God's people everywhere. Such works are greatly needed in an age of dangerous and futile efforts to harmonize the perfect written Word of God with materialistic theories of cosmic evolutionism. May our Lord be pleased to honor this document for his own glory in the hearts of many people.

John C. Whitcomb, Th.D.
1989

Preface

One of the best parts of teaching and giving seminars is the question-and-answer time. The speaker never knows what to expect! Although some questions arise often and others are brand-new, all questions are encouraging signs that the audience is thinking. Questions also help to keep a speaker humble—because no one has all the answers! This book is a collection of many such questions from both the Bible and astronomy. My thanks go to astronomy classes at Grace College and also to audiences of Bible-science seminars. Their questions and interest have encouraged my own study of God's grand universe.

Astronomy books are difficult to write because one must keep an ear tuned to the news. But many answers in this book are timeless, certainly true where Scripture is involved. I have tried to be tentative in areas where revision could occur and any corrections from readers or questions for a later edition would be appreciated. This revised edition is a thorough update of the original book. Ten new questions and answers have also been added.

Most astronomy books take an evolutionary and secular view of science. They often raise more questions than they answer. This study attempts to bring some balance to astronomy by presenting a Christian perspective. Literal creation days and a young age for the universe are also promoted because I believe this view is true to Scripture and science. I have not tried to be artificially spiritual with the answers. Not all the questions touch directly on Bible issues, but the entire universe is God's creation and all of astronomy proclaims this truth.

This book is intended as a resource for the classroom and home. The seven parts are a somewhat arbitrary division of subjects. Since many important astronomy questions are not addressed in this study, ideas from readers for future incorporation would be appreciated. Footnotes have purposely been omitted. Instead, references in the back are included for documentation of ideas and for further study. A short glossary with some basic astronomical terms is also included.

May this book help you to appreciate many details of the beautiful heavens as they declare the glory of God.

PART ONE

The Earth
and Moon

1. Is the earth at the center of the universe?

It is popular today to deny any special recognition for the earth. Scientists tell us that we live on a speck of dust, circling a humdrum star in a far corner of an obscure galaxy. While this may be true, the earth nevertheless remains of central importance. Scripture gives a refreshing contrast to secular thinking by declaring that the earth and mankind are not an insignificant result of accidental evolution. The Book of Genesis states that our planet was created three days before the sun, moon, and stars. The purposes of the stars relate directly to the earth: to provide a calendar system (Gen. 1:14) and to declare God's glory to men (Ps. 19:1). The earth is also a universal reference point in that Christ came here to walk among mankind and will one day return. An unseen spiritual battle goes on for the souls of men, focusing on this earth and extending to high places (Eph. 6:12). The earth is truly of spiritual and physical importance in the universe.

Once it was thought that the earth was physically located at the exact center of the universe and furthermore that it did not move. This "geocentric" view is still held today by some, although Scripture does not require it and observations clearly show the earth's movement. The earth rotates on its axis every 24 hours. It also revolves around the sun once a year. These motions add together in a dizzy combination. The earth's spin results in a surface speed of 1,000 miles per hour at the equator. The speed of the earth due to its orbital motion around the sun is 66 times greater still, 30 times faster than a rifle bullet. During an average person's lifetime of 70 trips around the sun, 41 billion miles are traveled. While you read this page, the earth has already traveled more than 1,000 miles! Fortunately, we do not directly notice this motion since the earth's faithful gravity force ensures that both its atmosphere and inhabitants remain firmly in place. However, the earth's motion is clearly shown by the westward movement of the sun, moon, and stars across the sky (see table 1).

We really don't know where the physical center of the universe is. Depending on the universe's actual geometry, there may be no unique central physical location. The question of the earth's physical position in space is less important than the spiritual reality of God's love for his people.

Table 1
Earth's Major Motions

Motion	Speed
Rotation on axis	1,000 miles/hour (at equator)
Revolution around the sun	66,600 miles/hour
Rotation of the Milky Way Galaxy	500,000 miles/hour
Overall motion of our galaxy through space	3.3 million miles/hour

2. Did Bible writers believe the earth was flat?

No—this false idea is *not* taught in Scripture. In the Old Testament, Job 26:7 explains that the earth is suspended in space, the obvious comparison being with the spherical sun and moon. As early as 150 B.C., the Greek astronomer Eratosthenes had measured the approximately 25,000-mile circumference of the earth. The round shape of our planet was a conclusion easily drawn by watching ships disappear over the horizon and also by observing eclipse shadows. We can assume that such information was well known to New Testament writers. The earth's spherical shape was, of course, also understood by Christopher Columbus. Some people of his day may have thought the earth was flat, but certainly not the great explorers. Bible critics have claimed that Revelation 7:1 assumes a flat earth since the verse refers to angels standing at the "four corners" of the earth. Actually, the reference is to the cardinal directions: north, south, east, and west. Similar terminology is often used today when we speak of the sun's rising and setting, even though the earth, not the sun, actually does the moving. Bible writers used the "language of appearance" just as people always have. Without it, the intended message would be awkward at best and probably not understood at all. When the Bible touches on scientific subjects, it is entirely accurate.

3. What causes leap year?

Leap year is needed in our calendar system because there is not an exact number of rotations of the earth (days) during one orbit around the sun (year). Instead, one earth orbit consists of 365 days, 5 hours, 48 minutes, 46 seconds, etc. Without any correction, the seasons would slowly move through the calendar months, and farmers could not depend on calendar dates for the planting of their crops. March would eventually occur during winter and August during spring. Adding one day—February 29—to the calendar every four years makes up for the extra time, and this has been done since 45 B.C., from the time of Julius Caesar. However, even this extra day every fourth year does not exactly solve the problem. Since the extra earth rotation is not quite 6 hours, a new formula was established in 1582 during the time of Pope Gregory. Century years, such as 2000 or 2100, only have February 29 added if they are divisible by 400. Thus A.D. 2000 and 2400 are leap years; A.D. 2100 and 2300 are not. This Gregorian calendar will keep the seasons assigned to the proper months for many thousands of years.

Why did God arrange an uneven number of earth rotations for each trip around the sun? Perhaps because he doesn't want us to take the calendar system for granted! Throughout history the calendar has required close monitoring and adjustment. Perhaps God is also showing us how important is every detail of his creation, not the least of which is the earth's motion.

---

4. Is the earth's magnetic field decreasing?

An ongoing decay of the earth's magnetism has been measured by magnetometers and satellites. Records show that over 150 years its strength has dropped by about 6 percent, a dramatic change, especially on a long-age time scale. If this decrease continues at the present rate, the earth's magnetic field could disappear completely in just 1000 to 2000 years. This has important implications since the earth's magnetic field protects us from harmful solar radiation. Without this field radiation-induced diseases would increase greatly all over the earth. Some have taken this weakening field as an indicator that world history is drawing to a close.

Has the earth's magnetic field decreased uniformly since the creation, or does it have a more complicated pattern of change? The question is difficult to answer because we do not really understand the source of the field. It arises in the earth's greatest depths, about which detailed information is lacking. Even with a recent creation, the 150 years of available data covers less than 3 percent of earth history. At present, the limited data indicates several historical reversals of the earth's magnetic field. These fluctuations may have occurred during the Genesis flood. At this time "all the springs of the great deep burst forth" (Gen. 7:11). This tectonic disturbance may have greatly altered the earth's magnetism. A straightforward view of the earth's magnetism sees it as a young-earth age indicator, established at creation, some thousands of years ago. Over time this field is gradually diminishing with additional fluctuations. Creationists eagerly await more magnetic data, either from past records or from new measurements, that will further refine our understanding of the earth's important magnetic field.

----

5. Is there a hole in the ozone layer?

The ozone layer is composed of triatomic oxygen molecules (O_3) located in the upper atmosphere, 12 to 18 miles high. These molecules provide an important protective shield against ultraviolet radiation from the sun. Ozone is very effective in absorbing the ultraviolet energy, and without such protection we would suffer from serious eye problems and a higher incidence of skin cancer. Ultraviolet light also damages plants and sea plankton. A seasonal degeneration of the ozone umbrella has been measured, mainly above Antarctica. It is uncertain whether these ozone changes are caused by man-made chemicals or result from natural processes. Although the effects of chemicals such as chlorofluorocarbons (CFCs) and jet exhaust are definitely destructive to ozone, it actually is surprising how tolerant to abuse the ozone layer and the entire atmosphere are. Given a chance to recover, these complex structures appear able to restore themselves.

There is some indication that periodic degeneration of the ozone shield may be partially caused by the sun itself. Solar wind particles follow the invisible lines of the earth's magnetic field into the Arctic and Antarctic regions. This solar radiation may temporarily destroy or redistribute some of the ozone. There seems to be a regular pattern of decreasing and increasing ozone over the years. As long as the ozone disturbance is small and remains limited to the polar regions, there is no great danger to the health of mankind.

---

6. Has the earth's tilt changed?

The polar axis of the earth is tilted at 23.5° from the vertical. This "leaning over" is responsible for our seasons (see figure 1). Writers such as Immanuel Velikovsky have suggested that the earth's axis tilt may have been different in the past and also that catastrophic collisions may have completely turned the earth over on its side. Such events would have produced drastic changes in the climate. On the basis of this hypothesis, ice caps would seasonally point directly at the sun and then in the opposite direction. The earth's ice would melt and refreeze on an enormous scale, resulting in major flooding and danger to life. Some of this

Figure 1
Earth's path around the sun
*Shown are the permanent tilt of the earth
and the four seasons in the Northern Hemisphere.*

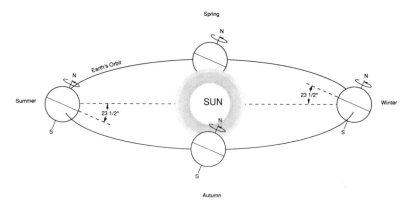

speculation is used to explain the fossil record, the Genesis flood, and other Old Testament catastrophes.

Did the earth's tilt really change in this way? No one can answer with certainty, but it seems doubtful for at least three reasons. First, since the collapse of the vapor canopy and tectonic activity is sufficient to explain the worldwide flood and the fossil record (see Question 60), a changing earth tilt is an unnecessary complication. Second, the regular seasons are cited in Genesis 8:22 as an example of God's faithfulness:

> "As long as the earth endures,
> seedtime and harvest,
> cold and heat,
> summer and winter,
> day and night
> will never cease."

Any shift of the earth's orientation would result in major changes of our seasons. An increased tilt would cause more

21

severe seasons; less tilt would tend to eliminate or reduce seasonal variation. Third, a temporary yet severe tilt of the earth's axis by a collision with some space object would have left permanent evidence that is not present today. For example, an elongated moon orbit would be expected to result from lunar gravity interaction with a colliding object. However, the moon's orbit deviates a mere 12 percent from a perfect circle.

Many novel ideas have been proposed to explain unusual events in the earth's history. Some are foolish, such as the belief that the pyramids were built by beings from outer space. Other ideas remain as interesting possibilities, such as a changing earth tilt. The Christian who is interested in earth history should be aware of these options. However, it is unwise to give undue emphasis to purely speculative areas.

7. Is the earth's temperature changing?

Data collected over many years shows that the earth's average temperature has remained very stable. In recent centuries it has changed at most by only about one degree. A greater worldwide change of just 4° to 5° F certainly would have major consequences. If it were a warming trend, the ice caps could melt and flood the coastal areas of the continents. Greenland and Antarctica might become newly uncovered real estate. On the other hand, a cooling trend would make living conditions in the far north and south even more severe than they already are. As the ice caps grew larger, ocean levels would drop and coastal shorelines would widen. There would be severe ecological consequences for every form of life on Earth.

Some scientists predict that the earth's temperature will increase by several degrees over the coming decades. The cause is said to be the great amount of carbon dioxide that man has put into the air by burning coal, oil, and natural gas. The CO_2 could become a blanket that traps solar energy at the earth's surface. This "greenhouse effect" is similar to what happens in a glass enclosure, such as a car with closed windows. Even on a cold day, sunshine will warm the interior of such a space. A few other scientists predict an opposite temperature trend on Earth since they believe that the sun may dim slightly and thus cool the earth. This happened from 1645 to 1710 and resulted in a period of cold weather over much of the world. A single year is not very significant in predicting change. The earth's climate changes slowly if at all and is usually defined as a 100-year average of the weather.

Which idea is the correct one for the earth's future, a warming or a cooling trend? Most likely neither of the opposing conditions will occur, and our stable climate will continue. Regarding carbon dioxide levels, the Creator has built strong controls into the earth's atmosphere and seas that counterbalance the buildup of chemicals. This is certainly not a license to abuse the land or sky, since everyone should have a great interest in preserving the integrity and health of the creation.

---

8. Is the Bermuda Triangle really a mystery?

An area off the east coast of Florida gets a lot of bad publicity! Many planes and ships are said to have mysteriously disappeared within this so-called Bermuda Triangle. Its corners are the southern Virginia coast, the Florida Keys, and Bermuda Island, covering about 14,000 square miles total. Sensational books have proposed that the lost city of Atlantis lies under the sea at this location—or that it is the site of an underwater flying-saucer base. As with UFO reports, a closer look at the Bermuda Triangle stories often reveals exaggeration or missing details. The most famous of these "mysteries" have commonsense explanations that are seldom heard. One interpretation involves the action of the Gulf Stream, which sweeps through this area of the Atlantic Ocean. Any downed plane or disabled ship in the triangle will rapidly drift northeast and out to sea, the result being an apparent disappearance of the vessel. The Bermuda Triangle region is a heavily traveled section of the ocean, through or above which pass hundreds of ships and planes every day without incident. Whenever there is a problem reported in the region, another fanciful story quickly starts concerning "supernatural happenings." Of course, not every Bermuda Triangle mystery has been solved. However, commonsense answers will most likely be found.

---

9. What are meteorites?

Meteorites are rocks that fall from the sky. They come from the space surrounding the earth, a region that is a shooting gallery of radiation and high-speed particles. Some of this space debris consists of the remnants of old, disintegrated comets. Other material results from past collisions between space material and the moon or nearby planets. Like a giant vacuum cleaner, the earth's gravity field sweeps up a path of this material as we circle the sun. There is a possible reference to a meteorite in Acts 19:35. Apparently an object that had fallen from the sky was worshipped in Ephesus, perhaps because it was thought to be supernatural.

Most of the falling fragments are completely melted in the 50-mile-high upper atmosphere. This results in streaks across the sky known as "shooting stars," or meteors. They are not really stars at all, but instead are nuggets of rock material, usually pebble-sized. The larger chunks of rock sometimes survive the heat and hit the ground, falling at the rate of about a dozen per day. These meteorites show signs of surface melting, and they are either stonelike or a metallic alloy of iron and nickel. Most land in the ocean; the ones hitting dry land quickly weather and blend in with normal rocks.

The most obvious meteorite crater in the United States is in Arizona. Nearly a mile wide and 600 feet deep, it was caused by a building-size meteorite that disintegrated upon impact, although fragments can still be found in the surrounding desert (see Question 104). A few years ago, two small meteorites hit a neighborhood in Connecticut. One smashed a mailbox; the other space rock punched through a house roof and landed in the dining room!

Several times each year there are dramatic meteor showers, occurring when the earth's orbit passes through a cloud of rock material. During such a shower, as in a slow-motion fireworks show, individual streaks of light cross the sky. These meteor showers are quite unpredictable in intensity. In November 1833, an intense meteor shower or storm occurred, called the Leonids, with hundreds of shooting stars seen per minute. Another well-known meteor shower, called the Perseids, takes place around August 12 each year. At this time there is about one meteor visible per minute, with the best viewing after midnight.

In a future day, many objects will fall from the sky (see Question 87). This includes a burning "star" called *Wormwood* that will cause great destruction and sorrow (Rev. 8:10–11). This may well be a large, blazing meteorite.

_____

10. What is a satellite?

In 1957, the Soviets put the first artificial satellite in orbit around the earth. It was called *Sputnik,* which means fellow traveler. Although it burned up as it reentered the atmosphere after only three months, this event launched the world into the space age. Early satellites were watched by many people and observation times were listed in newspapers. Now, hundreds of silent, graceful satellites cross the sky unnoticed each night. Some artificial satellites reflect the sun and look like slowly moving stars or nonblinking airplanes. Many move from west to east, while the polar satellites move in a north-south direction. The best time to see them is during the early evening, when satellites may pass overhead every ten minutes or so. Some of them tumble in flight and appear to flicker off and on as they reflect the sun. Of the approximately 10,000 space objects tracked by the government, two-thirds are known as "space garbage," such as dead satellites and spent rocket casings.

A satellite stays in orbit because of its great speed. If it somehow suddenly stopped, it would fall straight to the earth's surface. Satellites circle the earth under the control of our planet's gravity force, like a ball swung on the end of a string. The Space Shuttle flies 200 miles high and circles the earth about once every 100 minutes, but more distant satellites have longer orbit times. The geostationary satellites, at a distance of 22,300 miles, take exactly 24 hours to complete one earth orbit. Thus, when placed in orbit outward from the equator, they remain permanently over the same spot on Earth. These synchronous satellites must travel almost 7,000 miles per hour to keep up with the earth's spin. They are equivalent to a giant radio tower that reaches into space, one-tenth the distance to the moon. You can tell where they are in the sky by looking at television satellite antennae or dishes, which are aimed at them.

One additional satellite should be mentioned. It is the oldest, largest, best-known, and most useful satellite. This object is the moon, our only natural satellite. At a quarter-million miles from the earth, it completes one orbit each 29 ½ days (one lunar month). In comparison, all our space probes are tiny and insignificant. Man-made satellites are temporary, with orbits that decay sooner or later. What man sends up must eventually come down! However, the moon continues its 12 to 13 faithful cycles each calendar year, as it has done since it began on the fourth day of creation.

———————

11. Have scientists discovered the moon's origin?

Scientists have devised four major theories for the moon's beginning.

1. The *fission* theory states that the moon long ago split off from the spinning earth, like mud flung from a bicycle wheel. Some say that the Pacific Ocean basin is the scar that remains from this loss of material. There are four distinct problems with this theory. First, today's earth and moon do not have nearly enough circular motion for fission to ever have occurred. Second, although a moon splitting off from the earth would be expected to orbit directly above the equator, in actuality the moon's orbit is always tilted between 18° to 28° to the earth's equator. This is the reason why the moon appears higher or lower in the sky during different seasons. Third, while the fissioned moon was moving outward from the earth, gravity would have pulverized it into Saturn-type rings. Fourth, moon rocks are chemically different from the equivalent material on Earth. It does not appear that the moon came from the earth.

2. According to the *capture* theory, gravity brought the moon into permanent earth orbit when it once wandered too close to Earth. The main problem in this theory is the low probability that two large space objects would pass each other so closely. Another problem involves the actual "capture" mechanism—it simply wouldn't happen! Instead, the moon would continue on its journey. We have

often sent space probe "fly-bys" to other planets and they are not captured but instead are thrown outward with great speed, as in a crack-the-whip game. Finally, capture doesn't really qualify as an origin theory since it assumes the moon's prior existence.

3. The third theory has several names: *condensation, nebular contraction,* or *accretion.* It proposes the concurrent formation of both the earth and moon from clouds of space material. As a result, the new moon "just happens" to circle the earth. The main assumption here is that space material will actually fall together into a big lump due to gravity. Force calculations rule out such a collapse unless the cloud of material is already quite dense. Present-day dust clouds observed in space are rarely this dense, and most are spreading outward.

4. The fourth lunar-origin theory, very popular today, calls for a *collision* between the early earth and another large planetary object. The impact resulted in an orbiting cloud of debris that eventually grouped itself into the moon. Some critics of this theory believe that such a giant impact would totally melt the earth's crust. Others question the probability of another object hitting the earth with the precise speed and direction needed to result in the formation of the moon. Some computer models show that such a collision would result in two earth moons rather than just one, or even a Saturn-type ring. The main reason for promoting the collision idea appears to be that none of the other lunar-origin theories work.

It was hoped by many experts that the manned visits to the moon from 1969 to 1972 would provide definitive answers to the lunar-origin question. Instead, many new questions were raised, and the origin of the moon remains a mystery to secular science. One common idea in each of the four "natural" theories is that the moon formed by slow, random processes. Scripture is in direct contrast to

THE EARTH AND MOON

such reasoning—the moon was created suddenly (Ps. 33:6) and from nothing (Heb. 11:3).

---

12. What causes the tides?

Ocean tides provide an example of the moon's orderly and essential motion around the earth. Earth tides are caused primarily by the gravitational action of the moon. As the earth rotates, the moon causes two high tides and two low tides at a given location on the earth's surface every 24 hours. Tides are especially high when the moon phase is either new or full. At these times the sun's gravity also contributes to the tidal effect. When the moon is overhead, even the land areas are raised by several inches due to the moon's gravity influence. The solid earth is somewhat stretchable and can be pulled out of its round shape by the moon's gravity. If we could only hear the creaking and groaning of planet earth as it responds to the moon's pull!

The ocean tides are not an accidental or random result of solar-system formation, for they have great value in cleansing shorelines and helping ocean life to prosper. Tides provide an important component of the ocean currents. Without these currents, the oceans would stagnate along the seacoasts of the world and the death of marine life— both animals and oxygen-producing plants—would soon follow. Our very existence depends upon the moon's tidal regulation of this intricate food web (see also Question 15).

---

13. Why do we see only one side of the moon?

The moon rotates once on its axis during the very same period of time that it orbits the earth, 29 ½ days. Thus, as it circles the earth, it turns in synchronism, so that we always see the same face of the moon. This is not unusual for moons; many other solar-system moons are similarly "locked in" as they orbit their planets. Our own moon has slightly more mass on its near side, so gravity keeps the moon turning with this side facing toward the earth. The effect is similar to twirling a ball on a string. The tied side of the ball always faces inward.

It was not until the space probes of 1959 and 1960 that photos were taken of the moon's far side. An abundance of lunar craters was found and not as many smooth, dark areas as on the near side.

14. Does the moon appear every night?

No—each day the moon rises about 50 minutes later than the previous day. This means that half the time the moon rises in the sky during daylight hours. When it rises in the morning, it is not likely to be seen at all! Table 2 shows some approximate rising, overhead, and setting times for different moon phases. Israel's calendar during Old and New Testament times was based on these moon phases. A new month began when the waxing crescent phase (just after the new moon) was first observed. Watchmen were assigned to locate this young crescent moon. Festivals were also scheduled around these moon phases (Num. 10:10).

Table 2
Phases of the Moon

Phase	Rises	Overhead	Sets
New	6 A.M.	noon	6 P.M.
First Quarter	noon	6 P.M.	midnight
Full	6 P.M.	midnight	6 A.M.
Third Quarter	midnight	6 A.M.	noon

15. Do moon phases affect the earth?

One obvious effect of lunar phases is the tides, which are highest when the moon's phase is either new or full (see Question 12). Many people also believe that moon phases influence the weather, agriculture, and animal physiology and behavior. In some cultures special efforts are made to plant and harvest crops during the "correct" signs of the moon. Both the changing brightness of the moon and tidal action may indeed have a minor influence on farm crops and animal life. Studies have also tried to find a connection between moon phases and such things as birth rates and incidence of crime. Some have gone even further and used the moon to predict stock-market activity. The results are not very convincing. Some of the other effects, especially in farming, need more study.

16. What causes eclipses?

An eclipse of the moon occurs when the earth is lined up exactly between the sun and moon. The moon's phase must be full to move into this position. A *lunar eclipse* generally occurs at some earth location once or twice each year, and the event can last for several hours. The eclipsed moon appears to turn a red-brown color as the earth's shadow moves across the lunar surface. Alternately, when the moon moves between the sun and earth, a *solar eclipse* occurs (see figure 2). This happens at the time of the new-moon phase. Partial solar eclipses can be observed almost every year, but a total eclipse is very rare. It brings darkness to a small area of the earth and lasts for only a few minutes. At this time the sun's beautiful corona, or outer atmosphere, can be seen. Eclipses are unusual because the

31

Figure 2

Lunar and solar eclipses

*The positions of the sun, earth, and moon
are shown at the times of lunar (upper figure) and solar
(lower figures) eclipses. The dark areas represent shadows.
The figures are not drawn to scale.*

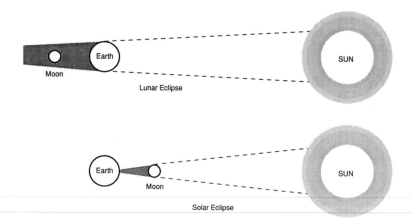

moon is usually located above or below the plane of the earth-sun system.

It may seem surprising that our moon is able to cover the sun completely during a solar eclipse since the moon is almost 400 times smaller in diameter than the sun. However, the moon is also almost 400 times closer to Earth, with the result that the sun and moon have the same apparent size in the sky. Among all the moons and planets in the solar system, this perfect match only occurs between the earth's sun and moon. As with all the details of God's creation, there is planning and purpose in eclipses. Since total solar eclipses are rare and very precisely specified in time, records of them have proven useful in assigning dates to events in history, including those recorded in the Bible. In an indirect way, eclipses serve as valuable "signs" to mark the days and years (Gen. 1:14).

A solar eclipse has been suggested by some secular scientists as the cause of the darkness that covered the land at the Lord's crucifixion. However, this supernatural darkness lasted for three hours, much longer than an eclipse (Matt. 27:45). It should also be noted that the Passover was held on the fourteenth day of the lunar "month" (Lev. 23:5), which was two weeks *after* the new moon, ruling out a solar eclipse. Neither could the Egyptian plague of darkness have been an eclipse (Exod. 10:23). The Exodus darkness lasted three days, and was more intense than that of an eclipse—yet "all the Israelites had light. . . ." One needs to resist the use of science to explain miracles. By one definition, a miracle is an exception to scientific law.

---

17. What does a ring around the moon mean?

A ring around the moon often means that rain or snow is near, but one must keep in mind the uncertainties of weather prediction. A halo sometimes surrounds the moon, especially during the full-moon phase. This halo is caused by cirrus clouds, which float three to six miles above the earth and consist of ice crystals. By day these clouds look like thin wisps or curls. At night they are too thin to hide the moon, but to us their reflection of the moonlight takes on the ring shape. Cirrus clouds often precede an approaching mass of moisture, which may or may not lead to precipitation. The next time you observe a bright ring around the moon, watch for a possible change in the weather.

---

18. What are the land and sky like on the moon?

Because the moon rotates once in 29 ½ days, the time between its sunrise and sunset lasts about two weeks. The moon's daylight temperature is around 200° F, with –200°F after dark. The bright regions on the moon's near side consist of rugged mountains and ridges between craters. The darker patches were originally mistaken by Galileo for oceans and still carry the name *maria* (pronounced mar'-ē-a), which is Latin for "seas." These regions are actually flat areas of basalt lava flows (see also Question 105).

Since there is no lunar atmosphere, the daytime sky is very different from the earth. Air is required to scatter the blue color of sunlight across the sky. With no air, the moon's daytime sky remains as black as night. The sun itself is visible, of course, but its light is like a large bright star in the night. The lack of lunar air also results in no clouds, no colorful sunsets or rainbows, and no wind or rain. "Shooting stars" never appear in the lunar sky, because there is no air to produce the friction that heats up meteors. Occasional meteorites hit the lunar surface and make small craters, but there is no sound to accompany them. The stars and planets shine steadily in the moon's sky with no twinkling, with the same stars and constellations seen from both the earth and the moon. The shift in position from earth to moon is not great enough to make any significant difference in the stars that are visible.

From the vantage point of the moon, the earth appears to hang motionless in the black sky. It shows different phases of light, but the earth neither rises nor sets. From the moon, the earth appears four times larger than the moon does to us. When astronauts were on the moon, the earth's oceans made it look like a lovely blue oasis in space.

---

19. Is there a problem with moon dust?

The problem—at least for some scientists—is a *lack* of lunar dust. If the moon is ancient it should have collected a considerable depth of space dust, the material that continually rains down from space onto the surfaces of both the earth and moon. Early estimates were as great as 14 million tons of space dust falling to the surface of the earth each year. On that basis, there would be an estimated lunar-dust accumulation of 60 meters during the 4.5 billion years of assumed lunar history. On the earth, this dust is rapidly moved around by wind and water, with much of it being swept into the sea. On the moon, however, erosion is very limited and there is no wind or precipitation of any kind. The moon should therefore collect a growing depth of dust and meteorite fragments. The manned Apollo trips to the moon showed only a thin layer (two to four inches) of moon dust. The astronauts did not sink into a deep sea of dust.

More recent measurements of dust accumulation from space give results as much as a thousand times less than originally thought. The early estimate of 60 meters of lunar dust thickness, when divided by 1,000, results in only about two inches of dust, in apparent agreement with the long-age view. There are two creationist responses to this. *First,* the evolutionary view predicts a much greater influx of dust in the early stages of the solar system. The hypothetical cloud of dust that formed the sun and planets should have been much thicker in the past. On this basis a thick layer of moon dust is still predicted, and it is still missing. *Second,* the revised value of a much smaller dust accumulation from space remains tentative. Scientists continue to make adjustments in their estimates of the meteor and space dust amounts that fall upon the earth and moon.

The history of the lunar dust problem can be briefly outlined as follows:

pre-1966   Some estimates postulated great depths of lunar dust.

1966	Unmanned *Surveyor* probes landed on the moon, showing little dust and a firm lunar surface.
1969	The first manned lunar landing *(Apollo 11)* showed just two to four inches of dust.
post-Apollo	Estimates of dust accumulation were greatly reduced. Another alternate view is that the thick lunar dust layer is actually present, but that it has been welded into rock by meteorite impacts.

The moon dust problem has not completely gone away. The lunar dust layer is thin, which fits recent creation more readily than it does the long-age view. Creationists await improved measurements of dust accumulations on the earth and moon.

PART TWO

The
Solar System

---

20. What makes up our solar system?

The ingredients of our solar system are:

One star (the sun)
Nine planets
Dozens of moons
Millions of asteroids and comets
Billions of meteors

Since the sun accounts for more than 99 percent of the total mass, it is definitely a *solar* system. Pluto's orbit provides the outer "border," giving an overall diameter in excess of 7 billion miles. A light beam crossing the solar system would require more than ten hours for the trip. Within the solar system, the planets circle the sun, and the moons in turn circle their respective planets. Gravitational attraction causes all the objects to move with clockwork perfection. The minor solar-system members—including asteroids and comets—are also held captive by the sun's gravity force. Table 3 shows how the solar system fits into space in general.

Table 3
Hierarchy of Space

Object	Diameter
Earth	7,900 miles
Earth-Moon orbit	478,000 miles
Sun-Earth orbit	186 million miles
Solar System	7 billion miles
Milky Way	100,000 light-years*
Known Universe	30 billion light-years (estimate)

*One light-year is about 6 trillion miles.

21. Has the origin of the solar system been determined?

The planets in our solar system are said to have originated either *from* the sun (fission), *independent of* the sun (capture), or *along with* the sun (nebula, accretion). Since these same three ideas also arise in current origin theories for the moon, the problems mentioned in Question 11 also apply to the solar system.

One version of the *fission* theory states that the sun was once sideswiped by another passing star and that huge portions of matter were torn loose from the sun and eventually coalesced into the present planets. However, a passing star could not easily provide the angular motion or momentum that the solar system possesses. *Capture* of planet material by the sun is a theory even less acceptable than fission. Gas clouds are present in space, but one can hardly imagine their capture by the sun's gravity. Most space clouds are very remote; they are isolated from stars by many light-years. *Nebular* formation of the planets requires the contraction of a gas cloud due to gravity, and the sun and planets then condense from the swirling cloud. There are two major problems with this idea. First, like a spinning ice skater who pulls her arms inward, contracting gas would have spun the sun up to a very rapid rotation. However, the actual rotation of the sun is much too slow to support this theory. The sun possesses only 2 percent of the solar system's circular motion or angular momentum. Gas clouds in space are generally observed to either spread out or to remain constant in size, not to contract. For a typical cloud, outward gas forces are much stronger than the inward pull of gravity.

Since every secular origin theory for the solar system begins with preexisting matter, none is really an *origin* theory at all! Aside from accepting supernatural creation from nothing (John 1:3; Col. 1:16–17), science must begin with material from an unknown source. Science alone will never have final answers regarding the true origin and purpose of the solar system. Only in Christ the Creator "are hidden all the treasures of wisdom and knowledge . . ." (Col. 2:3). This does not mean that we must abandon our search for scientific knowledge. It does mean that we must maintain a posture of reverence and spiritual humility in this search. After all, it is God's universe, and it reflects his attributes of perfect power, wisdom, and love.

---

22. Was the fourth day of creation 24 hours long?

According to Genesis 1:14–19, the sun, moon, and stars were made on the fourth day of the creation week. There have been many attempts to stretch the creation days into vast periods of time in order to accommodate Scripture with secular science. However, the problem is not with Scripture but with our attempts to rationalize and understand the creation week, something that cannot be done by finite minds! There are many details of God's creative plan that simply cannot be compromised with current scientific opinion. Some of the unanswered questions are:

1. How could plants exist on the third day, before the sun was present?
2. "Light" existed before the sun (Gen. 1:3). What light source did God use to mark the first three days?
3. Since the seas were also formed before the sun (Gen. 1:9–10), why didn't they quickly freeze? Why didn't the "water above" fall to the ground as snow (Gen. 1:9)?
4. Did the earth initially move in a straight line, or did it orbit the position of the yet-to-be-created sun?

An entire book could be filled with such questions from Genesis 1–2. All the answers would be speculative and probably wrong! The creation week was supernatural and therefore beyond our understanding. God has his own reasons for the order of creation events. We are in no position to question them or to offer suggestions for improvement! *Yes,* I believe that the days of creation were literal 24-hour time periods. Scholars have shown that this is the intended meaning of the text. The week of seven 24-hour days, so familiar to us, had its beginning at the creation. There is no object or motion in space with an obvious seven-day period, from which the week could have been derived naturally (see Question 102). God could have made everything in six microseconds or in 6 trillion years, but he chose literal days as a general pattern for mankind (Exod. 20:11). The literal creation days also display God's perfect glory and wisdom:

Does not wisdom call out? . . .
I was there when he set the heavens in place . . .
Then I was the craftsman at his side.
I was filled with delight day after day,
   rejoicing always in his presence.

Proverbs 8:1, 27, 30

23. What are the other planets like?

Let us consider a few distinctives of each planet in our solar system, in order of distance from the sun. *Mercury* is the fastest-moving planet. It makes a full revolution around the sun in just 88 days. Heavily cratered and without a trace of an atmosphere, Mercury looks much like our moon.

Venus has a surface that remains hidden beneath a permanent cloud cover. Some scientists once predicted that thick jungles and wildlife might be found on Venus, while others imagined a world completely covered by stormy seas. Space probes now have ended the guesswork regarding Venus. Its surface is covered with rocks, hills, and canyons. Any visitor would be poisoned by the carbon dioxide atmosphere, corroded by acid clouds, and crushed by immense air pressure equal to that of a half-mile depth of seawater. The visitor would also be cooked by the 900° F surface temperature and deafened by continuous thunder! Even though Venus is Earth's twin in size, its conditions are the opposite of Earth in almost every other way. We can conclude that no Venus life has evolved, nor could life exist if brought there from our planet.

Mars has a reddish appearance from iron oxides on its surface. It has a desert climate and ice caps consisting mostly of frozen carbon dioxide. The idea of Martian life remains popular, but evidence is completely lacking. Sev-

41

eral surface probes have landed on Mars and found a hostile world. Mars has a very thin atmosphere of carbon dioxide and oxygen and an average temperature of −76° F. There are dormant volcanoes; one called Olympus Mons towers 15 miles above the surrounding plain, three times higher than Mount Everest. The Valles Marineris Canyon is 4 miles deep and 60 miles wide, four times the size of the Grand Canyon. The *Pathfinder* probe in 1997 found evidence for historical floods on Mars, although the planet lacks moisture today.

Beyond the orbit of Mars lies the asteroid belt, a group of many thousands of rocks that orbit the sun. Some are pebble-sized; others resemble mountains flying through space. This debris is spread out over a gigantic ring that entirely circles the sun. It is not known whether these rocks were created in this form or are the result of some catastrophe in history, such as an exploding planet (which some scientists believe). One of the largest known asteroids has been named *Mathilde*. It appears to have a very light structure, similar to Styrofoam in density.

Jupiter is the largest planet, weighing as much as 318 Earths. It circles the sun nearly half a billion miles beyond Earth's orbit and has at least 16 moons. A small telescope shows the four largest moons of Jupiter as bright dots alongside the planet. Two pink cloud bands on Jupiter's surface can also be seen. They are composed of a variety of poisonous gases. The weather report from this hostile world is not pleasant: magnetic storms, crushing air pressure, and radiation showers. Obviously there are no plans for a manned visit to Jupiter! Even if we could go, there would be no place to land, since Jupiter does not have a solid surface like the earth. Instead, Jupiter is a sphere of thick, swirling gas, as are all the large outer planets. The most famous surface feature of Jupiter is its great red spot. This hurricane-like swirl of reddish chemicals has been observed for centuries. It alone is several times the size of Earth.

Saturn, the second largest planet, is best known for its beautiful halo of rings, which are 160,000 miles wide, and are composed of rocks and frozen chemicals, such as ammonia. There are actually hundreds of narrow individual rings, some of which are kept in place by small "shepherd moons" orbiting between them. Astronomers find it incredible that such intricate detail has remained in place for millions or billions of years, although an evolutionary view of long ages leaves little choice. One moon of Saturn, Titan, was once postulated to have evolved life on its surface, since—among other things—Titan has an atmosphere and a large size. However, studies have found mostly nitrogen there, along with some poisonous methane and cyanide. This mixture produces smog with a surface temperature near –300° F. There may be seas of liquid methane and icebergs of frozen nitrogen on Titan, but there is definitely no abundant life!

Uranus shines with a blue-green color due to its methane atmosphere. This planet has a dim halo of five narrow rings and is tipped over on its side. Miranda, one of Uranus's 17 known moons, was studied by *Voyager* in 1986. Its unusual details caused one astronomer to call it "the moon designed by a committee"! Marking the moon's surface are great oval patterns of grooves, looking like furrows in a field. At Miranda's equator is a 12-mile-high giant cliff. Any astronaut who slipped off such a cliff would fall for ten minutes before hitting bottom!

Neptune, four light-hours out from the sun, takes 165 years for each orbit. A person born there would not live long enough for one Neptunian birthday. The planet's surface temperature remains around –328° F. Neptune has a light blue color resulting from light absorption by methane gas in its atmosphere.

Pluto is the smallest and outermost planet, circling the faraway sun in perpetual darkness. If this remote planet has any atmosphere, the gases probably cover the ground as a snowlike coating. Pluto has a single moon called Charon. Future space probes will certainly reveal many more surprises that await detection in the far reaches of the solar system.

One conclusion from solar system studies is that its physical extremes are almost beyond imagination. The great variety in color, temperature, and surface detail effectively rules out any simple, secular origin theory. Every scientific theory of science is based on patterns of regularity, but—beyond the basic laws of motion—each planet has been found to be unique and unpredictable in appearance. A second conclusion about origins relates to the lack of life on other planets. God has apparently chosen to place life on Earth and nowhere else in the solar system. And life has certainly not evolved anywhere else on its own. The earth is truly to be enjoyed and appreciated for the many unique comforts provided for us. There is simply no other place quite like the "home" that has been created for us!

---

24. What are other moons like?

The earth's moon is just one of many satellites that circle the planets in our solar system. Pluto, too, has one large moon called Charon. Mercury and Venus have none, while Mars has two small moons that are shaped somewhat like giant potatoes. The other planets may have dozens each, and the known total for the solar system is now more than 60. This is an area of current research and the number of observed moons will surely increase.

Space probes have revealed that each moon has its own unique details. For example, Jupiter's four largest moons illustrate artistic variety. They were discovered by Galileo in 1609 and have been studied closely in recent years. The moon *Io* is brightly colored in oranges and reds, with at least eight active volcanoes. Sulfur compounds expelled by these volcanoes have filled a doughnut-shaped region that surrounds Io's orbit around Jupiter. On Io's surface are lakes of molten sulfur, or brimstone, reminding one of the "fiery lake of burning sulfur" described in Revelation 19:20. Jupiter's moon *Europa* is white in color with an icy surface marked by dark narrow fractures and towering icebergs. It looks somewhat like a cracked egg. There is much speculation about a possible salty ocean beneath this moon's crust, including submerged life forms. *Ganymede* has a strangely grooved terrain, as if a giant comb was dragged across the surface. *Callisto* is the most heavily cratered object known in the solar system. Its covering layer of fractured ice is an incredible 60 to 100 miles thick. One giant crater on Callisto looks like a bull's-eye target, with ten outer rings of mountain ridges as large as the entire Midwest. The many solar system planets and moons are not uniform in either color or surface features as a common spontaneous origin might predict. Instead, each uniquely shows God's creative imagination.

---

25. Is there a tenth planet?

Although it's doubtful, there may be a tenth planet in our solar system. The motion of Pluto, the outermost planet, has shown possible evidence of gravity from a remote object beyond it. This yet-unidentified object could turn out to be planet number ten, with still others beyond. Neptune and Pluto were themselves discovered by noting their gravity effect on nearer planets. Space-age exploration has verified the vast size of the universe and the infinite variety of its created entities. Creationists assert that space objects are all made for God's own pleasure (Col.

1:16), including any planets in the solar system that are beyond the present range of telescopes (see Question 27).

You may have wondered about the names of planets. With the exception of the earth, all are named after Greek or Roman deities. Any new planets or moons will surely be named in the same way, since rules for such names have been established by the International Astronomical Union. It is a sad paradox that God's handiwork in the heavenly realm is named for pagan gods. The apostle Paul faced this same insult in his day. Acts 28:11 explains that Paul sailed to Rome on a ship that had as its figurehead Castor and Pollux. These were Greek deities (as well as prominent stars), but the writer of Acts chose not to make an issue of this problem.

---

26. Do all the planets ever line up?

Every few years the idea arises that the planets are about to become perfectly aligned in their journeys around the sun. It is then usually predicted that this special situation will cause severe earthquakes and perhaps signal the end of the world. Since Jupiter is the largest planet, this event is sometimes called the Jupiter Effect. There is no factual basis for the Jupiter Effect story.

The nine known planets circle the sun at different distances and speeds, and occasionally two or three will appear to approach each other in a *conjunction*. Actually, of course, they remain millions of miles apart. To determine when all nine planets will gather to the same spot in the sky, one needs to calculate the least common multiple of their orbit times, which is well over a trillion years. And by then, chaotic motion will have invalidated the calculation. In other words, as far as we know, all of the planets will *never* line up! Even if the planets did somehow align themselves, there would be no resulting destruction on the earth. Planetary distances simply are too great for one planet to exert a significant gravity pull on another.

Two lessons can be learned from the Jupiter Effect story. First, science cannot predict a date for the end of the world—"No one knows about that day or hour, not even the angels in heaven, nor the Son, but only the Father" (Matt. 24:36). The second lesson relates to the first: False claims should never be used to bolster biblical truths, especially since Scripture does not need any supporting help.

----

27. Do other planets exist beyond the solar system?

This is an important question because life, if it exists elsewhere, could only be found on planets or their moons. Those who are confident that many life forms exist in space have proposed that there are millions of other planets in the Milky Way Galaxy alone. In recent years there have indeed been indications of planets around several nearby stars. These results are tentative because the distant planets themselves cannot be seen in the glare of starlight. Instead one notices a slight vibration of a star, presumably resulting from the gravity of an orbiting planet. In every case so far the indirect evidence shows the new planets to be massive, very hot, and probably gaseous. This description also fits a type of small star called a brown dwarf. Whether or not other planets exist, two things are certain. First, the earth is a special planet, with no other known location comparable to our created home. Second, there is no evidence that life exists elsewhere in the solar system or in space beyond.

47

28. What do we learn from comets?

Comets have given rise to many unusual ideas. Centuries ago it was believed that these "stars with tails" were signs of trouble on Earth: wars, plagues, and the like. British astronomer Fred Hoyle has proposed that comets are to blame for outbreaks of flu and smallpox. He believes that comets, sometimes unseen, swing by the earth and drop loads of germs on us from their tails. Hoyle assumes, of course, that comets contain microbes, but—in reality—no life has been detected on comets.

Comets may have a mixed reputation, but they silently continue to orbit the sun and they put on occasional majestic displays for us in the night sky. Each year, dozens of comets loop the sun. About one half of them have been named and studied on previous orbits; others are new.

Figure 3

The orbit of Halley's comet

At its most distant position the comet is three billion miles from Earth. At its smallest distance from the sun the comet moves inside the orbits of Mars and Earth (unlabeled planets). The open circle at the center of the figure represents the sun.

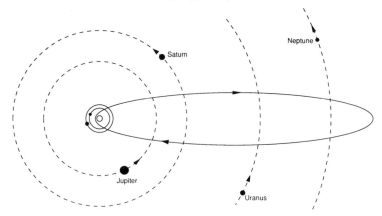

Seeing these comets usually requires binoculars, as well as patience. Comets don't last forever; sooner or later they may be ejected from the solar system or else disintegrate into separate pieces. There are clouds of dust in the solar system that are the ghosts of comets past. When the earth happens to move through such a cloud, it sweeps up some of this comet dust. Then we see "shooting stars," a repeat of the comet's original light show (see Question 9). In 1994, Comet Shoemaker-Levi was destroyed when it collided with Jupiter. The gravity of this massive planet actually protects the earth from similar collisions.

This raises a very basic question about comets—why are there any left? On a time scale of billions of years, they should all be long gone, either by melting, collision, or by escaping from the solar system. The average number of solar revolutions before a comet dissipates is estimated to be about 40 trips. Comet Halley has already been observed through 28 orbits, dating back to 240 B.C. Its remaining years are definitely numbered!

Astronomers recognize two comet varieties, with either short or long revolving periods. The short-period comets have orbit periods less than about 200 years. Halley's comet is an example, with a period of about 76 years. Long-period comets may require thousands of years for each solar pass. The origin of both kinds of comets remains a mystery. It is suggested that comets formed long ago near the outer planets. An unseen *Kuiper belt* of comets is thought to still exist there. It is further guessed that some of these Kuiper comets eventually move outward far beyond the known solar system to a vast *Oort cloud* of comets. A passing star then disturbs this outer comet cloud from time to time, deflecting new comets in toward a rendezvous with the sun. In this way the supply of fresh solar system comets is thus indefinitely renewed. The existence of the Kuiper belt and the Oort cloud of comets has not been verified. Perhaps there is an alternative: The presence of comets may be evidence that the solar system is not nearly as old as is often assumed.

Comets teach us two valuable lessons. First, they provide us with a vivid object lesson concerning the rapid erosion and decay of the universe. All physical objects are temporary and fading, including comets. Second, God's heavenly handiwork demonstrates his infinite power and glory. The exact motions of the comets, planets, and stars are sufficient proof of God's controlling presence.

---

29. Did a comet kill the dinosaurs?

There have been dozens of dinosaur extinction theories. Some of the suggested astronomy events include the following:

The sun became either too warm or too cool for dinosaur health.

A nearby supernova flooded the earth with deadly radiation.

The earth's magnetic field reversed direction, and the resulting incoming radiation was fatal to life.

A passing comet seeded the earth's atmosphere with poisonous chemicals.

One particular extinction theory has gained wide acceptance since the 1980s. It involves the impact of a large meteorite, asteroid, or comet with the earth. The collision is said to have occurred about 65 million years ago at the end of the geologic Cretaceous period. There resulted worldwide fires, tsunami or tidal waves, and violent storms with acid rain. The scenario further pictures great clouds of dust, soot, and smoke resulting from the catastrophe.

This material blocked sunlight on the earth for several months or years. Plants ceased their growth, and dinosaurs gradually diminished from the resulting collapse of food chains worldwide.

Scientists have offered two lines of evidence for such a catastrophic event. First, small amounts of the element iridium are found embedded in the clay layer located at the Cretaceous boundary. Iridium is often associated with space material. Thus it is suggested that the iridium was spread across the earth at the time of the collision. Second, scientists have identified a possible, large buried crater near the Yucatan Peninsula of Mexico. This crater has been dated at 65 million years old, just when the dinosaurs are assumed to have disappeared.

Several cautionary statements should be made. First, the element iridium also accompanies volcanic activity. The material does not necessarily come from beyond the earth. Second, the underground Yucatan structure is not known with certainty to be an actual crater. There are many such "cryptocrater" formations of unknown origin scattered across the earth. Third, why did the alleged impact kill off the dinosaurs while many other creatures remained healthy? Some of the least mobile creatures (tortoises, crocodiles) and also those most sensitive to environmental change (birds, fish) are still with us today.

Certainly there have been occasional impact collisions between the earth and space objects. However, creationists suggest that most dinosaurs died out as a result of the great flood of Genesis 6–8. Dinosaur representatives that were protected on the ark probably faced severe climate changes in the centuries following the flood, just a few thousand years ago. Creation research continues to demonstrate the importance of the worldwide flood in explaining earth history.

30. Did natural catastrophes shape our world's destiny?

Immanuel Velikovsky (1895–1975) was a Russian-born writer, trained in medicine and psychology. He developed many original and novel ideas regarding the history of the solar system and mankind (see also Question 6). In particular, he believed that major catastrophes have shaped the earth and planets, thus challenging the idea that slow changes in the present are the key to the past. Because he went against the grain of current scientific opinion, his views were rejected by contemporaries. Mavericks in science or in any other field often face emotional opposition from the establishment. Velikovsky wrote several books—including *Worlds in Collision* (1950), *Ages in Chaos* (1952), and *Earth in Upheaval* (1955)—and his popularity as an original thinker and underdog has grown in recent years.

Velikovsky's ideas are a mixture of truth and error. His proposal of a recent Ice Age is shared with creationists, as are his challenges to "the doctrine of uniformity" (that rates of formation and erosion have always been constant). However, Velikovsky is hardly a friend of creationists or Christians in general since he fully accepted evolutionary theory. Velikovsky denied the Genesis flood and attempted to explain away the Old Testament miracles as natural catastrophes. He made so many astronomical predictions that some of them were bound to prove correct. For example, he suggested that Jupiter must produce strong radio signals, and the signals were then discovered a year later. However, Velikovsky also claimed that Venus clouds were rich in carbon and dust, yet Venus probes have shown this idea to be entirely incorrect. Velikovsky was a brilliant scientist and some of his views show good insight. Although his writings are valuable for study, he was certainly as fallible in his thinking as anyone.

31. What powers the sun?

The dominant view of scientists is that nuclear fusion provides the sun's energy. Accordingly, hydrogen is converted to helium, releasing some of the vast energy stored within the nucleus. Along with heat and light, the fusion process should also produce a multitude of subatomic particles called neutrinos. The hydrogen-helium reaction is thought to occur at such a rapid rate that the earth should be continually flooded with these neutrinos. Theoretically, every square inch of the earth's surface should be hit by a trillion neutrinos each second, day and night! These neutrinos, if measured, would be the best evidence that nuclear fusion is indeed occurring within the sun. *But here we face a major problem in astronomy,* since neutrino detectors do not find neutrinos in sufficient numbers to agree with this nuclear theory. As a result, some scientists question whether nuclear fusion is the sole energy source for the sun. In effect, we are not absolutely certain what makes the sun shine!

The main scientific alternative for explaining the sun's energy is called "gravitational collapse" (see Question 99). That is, if the sun is slowly contracting, great amounts of energy would be released. Efforts to measure a changing solar diameter are so far inconclusive, but the chief argument used against the gravity source for the sun's energy is that the time scale required is "too short." Gravity collapse could keep the sun hot for only a few million years at most, whereas fusion could go on a thousand times longer. The long-age framework of modern evolutionary thinking has strongly biased the view of solar energy. Solar energy may actually come from a combination of both gravity and nuclear effects.

The sun is an average star, the only star that we can study closely. And yet we do not fully understand what powers it! This bears testimony to man's limited understanding of his nearest neighbors, let alone the entire universe beyond.

---

32. Is the sun shrinking in size?

A gradual decrease in the sun's diameter should be expected if solar energy is partially due to gravitational collapse (see Questions 31 and 99). For example, a change of radius of about 80 feet per year would be necessary to produce all of the sun's actual energy. Astronomers have attempted to measure changes in solar size for many years, but the procedure is extremely difficult. Vibrations of the sun and month-to-month irregularities of the solar surface can completely mask the effect. Although present data does not clearly show a shrinking sun, perhaps eclipse records will eventually help answer the question. Meanwhile, the possibility of a slowly contracting sun remains.

---

33. What causes an aurora?

Contrary to common belief, the northern lights—or *aurora borealis*—are not a reflection of sunlight off the polar ice caps. If this were true, we would see the lights continually. Instead, an aurora is a form of radiation made visible. It begins with protons and electrons that are boiled off the surface of the sun. Within just a few hours these high-speed particles reach the vicinity of the earth. They are potentially dangerous to our health, but they do not hit the earth directly. Instead, the earth's magnetic field deflects these particles and sweeps them into the polar regions. As this radiation hits the upper atmosphere, molecules of air begin to glow with energy. The northern lights often take the form of waving curtains of pastel colors. Some of the radiation is also sent to the Antarctic region, creating a display of southern lights *(aurora australis)*. Since both the northern and southern polar regions are largely uninhabited, the radiation hazard to the earth is minimized.

The farther one travels north of the equator, the brighter and more frequent the auroral display becomes. The activity actually occurs in a donut-shaped region around the magnetic pole, 60 to 600 miles high. The "donut" grows or shrinks according to the amount of incoming solar radiation. Northerners often speak of the beauty of the light display, and some have reported that the aurora seems to make a crackling or tingling sound on frigid nights. This type of strong solar activity can also affect worldwide radio communication.

The best chance to see an auroral display occurs about every 11 years (e.g., 2001, 2012), when the sun is extra active in its production of radiation particles. For reasons unknown, our sun goes through a very active period on an approximate 11-year schedule. Then the sun becomes speckled with dark blemishes called sunspots (see Question 34). At this time there is also an increase in the number of solar flares, a form of surface explosion. Accompanying this activity is an increase in solar radiation. These details are all part of the complexity of the solar furnace.

---

34. What are sunspots?

When Galileo studied these dark specks on the surface of the sun in 1610, he thought that they might be openings into the sun's interior. Actually, sunspots are whirlpools of particles that are stirred up by intense electrical and magnetic fields. The spots appear dark because they are 30 percent cooler than the rest of the sun's surface, although they still are about 4000° C, hotter than molten metal. Many sunspots are larger than the entire earth's diameter. They can best be seen by projecting the sun's image through a telescope onto a flat surface. Over several days the spots are seen to move across the solar surface, which demonstrates the sun's turning motion.

Sunspot numbers pass through a maximum about every 11 years. During this time the sun is covered with scores of spots, although at other times there may be none at all. The reason for this cycle of activity is not understood. The next good viewing of sunspots is expected to occur around 2001 or 2002 and again during 2012 or 2013. When at maximum numbers, sunspots have a number of effects on the earth. Associated with the spots are large solar eruptions called flares. These explosions eject electrons, protons, and ions into space. When they reach the earth, they cause an increase in the aurora, visible in the far north and south (see Question 33). The particles can also cause radio-TV reception to skip over long distances. Magnetic compasses can be affected, as can telephone communications. Less clear is the connection between sunspots and the world's climate. It has been observed in the past that reduced sunspot activity seems to lead to drought and lower temperatures. For example, from 1645 to 1710 there occurred what is called the Little Ice Age, when worldwide temperatures dropped by several degrees (see Question 7). This time of severe weather coincided with a protracted period of sunspot absence. Similarly, the "dustbowl" years of the 1930s occurred during a period of few sunspots. How dependent we are on the slightest changes in our nearest star!

35. Can we explain the "long days" of Joshua and Hezekiah?

Joshua 10:12–14 tells the story of the day when the sun—and time—stopped. The Israelites were fighting the Amorites in Canaan. During the battle, Joshua prayed for the sun and moon to stop, so he would have extra daylight to finish the task. Scripture records that his prayer was answered: The sun "delayed going down about a full day" (v. 13). The very objects in the sky that the Amorites worshipped fought against them!

Several modern interpretations of the story have been suggested. Some scholars say there was no actual miracle, but only the use of poetic language. The Israelites had fought so hard that it just seemed like two days of work in a row! Others propose that a cloud shaded the sun, keeping the day cool enough for the fighting to continue all through the afternoon. However, this relief from the heat would have benefited the enemy as much as Israel. Similarly, a solar eclipse has been suggested as causing reduced sunlight. But eclipses of the sun last for only a few minutes, not a whole day. All of these explanations fall far short of the statement that there has never been another day like the one described (Josh. 10:14; cf. Hab. 3:11). What *really* happened on that special day? As with all miracles, it is futile to speculate with scientific theories. The details are unclear, but we know that God could have refracted the light, or slowed the earth's rotation, or stopped the entire universe—all with equal ease!

Time stopped for Joshua, and it ran *backwards* for Hezekiah (2 Kings 20:9–11). God used this event as a special sign to show Hezekiah that he would regain his health. The sun's shadow moved backwards by ten steps, probably five to six hours on the sundial. That is, the sun appeared to move eastward instead of westward. The conclusion is again the same, that such a miracle is beyond scientific explanation. God may have temporarily reversed the earth's rotation, including all its inhabitants, or the miracle in Hezekiah's day could have been local instead of worldwide. The latter view is supported by 2 Chronicles 32:31, which describes envoys who traveled to the land where the miracle occurred. Joshua and Hezekiah both made lofty requests of the Lord, that the very heavens might be altered. And God answered their prayers. The sun, moon, and stars obey the Creator who placed them in the sky by the power of his word.

-----

36. Have computers discovered the biblical "long days"?

The report that computers have discovered the biblical "long days" of Joshua and Hezekiah continues to circulate *but is unfounded.* It is challenged here because false ideas should never be used to "support" Scripture. Furthermore, the computer story appears to raise modern science to a level of certainty that it simply does not possess.

As printed in tracts and magazines, the story describes a problem that scientists faced in the space program. Apparently a missing day turned up in the computer positions for the sun and moon over the past centuries. These celestial bodies were not quite where they belonged! The key to the problem was then found in the Old Testament. Mathematical corrections were needed for the "long days" of Joshua and Hezekiah (Josh. 10:13; 2 Kings 20:11). These events, when fed into the computer, then made everything turn out exactly right. Although this apparent verification of Scripture makes a very interesting story, computers are not this smart! The only way to determine a change in location of the sun or moon is to know their exact positions *prior* to the change, but there is no such reference point available. We do not know exactly the positions where the created sun and moon were first placed in the sky. Even eclipse records do not prove useful in solving the problem. Neither NASA nor any other space agency can confirm the computer story.

Can we not conclude that the long day of Joshua occurred exactly as described? And also that the backward motion of the sun in Hezekiah's time was a literal sign of God's power? Computers are neither needed nor able to prove these Old Testament events scientifically.

PART THREE

The
Stars

---

37. What is a star?

The sun is an "average" star, so it provides a good example for descriptive purposes. The majesty of the sun is nearly incomprehensible. It is an immense ball of seething gases, 864,000 miles in diameter. This is nearly four times the earth-moon distance. If the sun could be hollowed out like a giant basketball, a million planet Earths would easily fit inside, like so many marbles. But the sun is not hollow. Instead, an internal temperature of millions of degrees results from its furnace of nuclear reactions. (Note that I am using "nuclear fusion" to illustrate the magnitude of solar energy, but see Question 31 and 99 for further discussion.) Hydrogen fuses into helium with a release of energy and a loss of mass. In the sun, trillions of hydrogen atoms must disappear continually. Since about eight billion tons of solar material are converted entirely into energy each second, the sun is losing weight, moment by moment. As a result of this process, each square inch of the sun's surface shines with the intensity of 300,000 candles. This incredible energy production goes on day and night, summer and winter. Only one billionth of the sun's energy output actually hits the earth. The rest streams off into all directions of space. In just one second, the sun releases more energy than mankind has produced since the creation, including all the engines, power plants, and weapons ever constructed. And yet the "fuel guage" for the sun's energy supply remains on "full." Its energy reserves are nearly inexhaustible. The dramatic energy output of the sun illustrates what is also happening at this moment on innumerable other stars throughout our galaxy and the entire universe. There is no energy shortage on the part of these beautiful lights in the night sky, "the work of your [God's] fingers" (Ps. 8:3).

There are hazards involved in living close to this star as we do. Along with the sun's pleasant light and necessary warmth, dramatic explosions on the solar surface also bathe the earth in radiation. However, we are providentially protected from harm by multiple levels of safety shields. For example, when x-rays and gamma radiation from the sun (the most deadly solar output) collide with molecules high in the earth's atmosphere, the radiation energy is absorbed and broken down to a harmless level. Solar ultraviolet radiation is stopped by the ozone layer, 12 to 18 miles above the earth's surface. High-speed fragments of atoms, also called solar wind, are deflected by the earth's magnetic field away from populated areas, toward the far north and south regions of the planet. Finally, the 93-million-mile distance that separates us from the sun also insulates us from harm. If this expanse was not a vacuum, the explosive sounds of the hot sun would deafen us. If the earth-sun distance were less, the raging solar inferno could entirely vaporize the earth. The multiple safety features provided by God result in our safely enjoying the pleasant morning light from the sun.

38. Is every star different?

Even though there are more than 10^{22} known stars in the universe, each one is unique. No two stars have exactly the same properties. This may sound like guesswork, since we have analyzed very few stars in detail, but the conclusion is a certainty. A star has so many variables in its makeup that the probability of two identical stars is zero. These variables include the total number of atoms, exact chemical composition, size, temperature, and motion. Some stars show obvious color and brightness differences. Others require spectroscopic study to detect their particular identity or fingerprint.

Similarly, it is also true that every snowflake, blade of grass, and grain of sand is unique. They may all look alike but they're not identical. On the microscopic level there is practically an infinite number of ways to arrange atoms. Even a single snowflake, for example, has about 10^{20} atoms to arrange within itself! Every individual object in the universe, no matter how large or small, shows God's distinct creative glory and artistry. The same is also true, of course, for every person on Earth.

39. How many stars are known to exist?

On a clear, moonless night about 3,000 stars are visible with the unaided eye. A small telescope will increase the number to around 100,000 stars. But this is just the beginning! The stars we can easily see are all in our corner of the Milky Way Galaxy. The entire galaxy numbers about 100 billion stars. And beyond the Milky Way are other galaxies with many shapes and sizes. Around 100 billion such galaxies are known to exist. Taking the Milky Way as an average galaxy, the total number of known stars is thus $(100 \text{ billion})^2 = (10^{11})^2 = 10^{22}$. These estimated stars number 10,000,000,000,000,000,000,000, when we write this number out. This figure would be pronounced as "ten billion trillion" stars.

Suppose these stars were divided up among the world's total population of 6 billion people. Then each person on Earth would receive more than 1 ½ trillion stars! Yet all these stars may be only page one in God's catalog of the heavens. New instruments continue to probe deeper into space, with no end in sight. What an excellent way for the Creator to show his glory! Whatever the number he has created, God calls all the stars by name, and he keeps count of them (Ps. 147:4; Isa. 40:26).

---

40. How are star distances measured?

Since radar and space probes cannot reach the stars, other methods are needed for finding stellar distances. Nearby stars are measured with *parallax,* which involves two measurements of the star's exact position in the sky. The readings are taken on opposite sides of the earth's orbit, six months apart. From this triangulation (or surveying) method, the star distance is determined. In figure 4, the parallax angle is exaggerated. It is always smaller than one second of arc, less than 0.0003 degrees. The parallax technique works for stars out to a distance of several thousand light-years (ly). (See Question 74 for the definition of a light-year.) The satellite *Hipparchus,* launched in 1997, has been used for many of these measurements. Many thousands of stars fall within parallax range, including Arcturus (37 ly), Sirius (8.6 ly), and Spica (220 ly).

For the longer star distances, indirect methods are used. The Cepheid variable technique is useful out to millions of light-years. Cepheids are a category of stars whose ac-

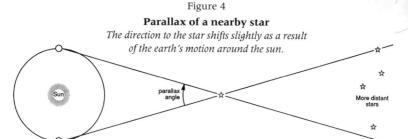

Figure 4

Parallax of a nearby star

*The direction to the star shifts slightly as a result
of the earth's motion around the sun.*

tual brightness is well known. If a Cepheid appears dim
its distance thus can be estimated. The method is similar
to judging the distance to an oncoming car by observing
its headlights in the distance. Cepheids are very bright
stars, so they can be identified in faraway galaxies. The
Cepheid method gives the distance to the Magellanic
Clouds (180,000 ly) and also to the Andromeda Galaxy
(2.9 million ly).

The final yardstick for stellar distances that will be mentioned here is the redshift of starlight (see Questions 63
and 66). This shift results from the overall expansion of
the universe. A star's light is altered as the star is carried
outward by the expansion of space. The effect is somewhat similar to water waves stretched out behind a speed-
boat. The term *redshift* arises because red is the color of visible light with the largest wavelength. Entire galaxies
appear to be receding from the earth, as measured by their
redshift. The faster they are traveling, the farther away
they seem to be. There is considerable guesswork in de-
termining actual distance from this redshift, and there are
also other possible explanations besides motion. If it is correct, this method gives distances for galaxies out to 15 billion light-years or more. Astronomers also use several
other distance techniques for stars. Although the parallax

distances are accurate to within about 10 percent, all other methods are more uncertain. Actual star distances could be somewhat smaller or larger than current estimates.

_____

41. How do we know what stars are made of?

Indeed, how can we study the stars at all? After all, it will probably be centuries if not millennia before any space probe reaches a star. Even when viewed through the largest telescopes, all stars remain tiny pinpoints of light and simply cannot be magnified in size as planets can. However, each twinkling light carries a detailed message that astronomers have learned to decipher. Much as one can look through a glass prism to see the rainbow colors of light, careful study shows that every star bears a unique "fingerprint" or spectrum in its light pattern. This spectrum reveals such information as the chemical composition of the stars. Most stars are found to be made of the common gases hydrogen and helium. The light from stars also reveals their surface temperatures. Some stars are just a few thousand degrees and have a yellow tint in the night sky. Hotter stars are blue or white in color and measure about 25,000 degrees. Starlight can also help determine the mass or weight of a star, and the results are astonishing. Gravity has squeezed some stars down to such a dense material that a handful of stardust would easily weigh more than all the buildings and vehicles in a large city. One especially dense type is called a neutron star or pulsar. If the five Great Lakes could be squeezed down to a neutron star's density, all the water would fit in a kitchen sink. Of course, the 20 trillion tons of condensed water would be hard on the plumbing; in fact it would quickly plunge to the center of the earth! Hundreds of neutron stars have been observed, but they are well removed from the earth. This is fortunate: If the earth was located near such a collapsed star, gravity could quickly tear our planet apart.

Additional information from starlight includes the magnetism, motion, size, and distance of individual stars. Astronomers are kept very busy analyzing this constant flow of data. The Lord's creation is very complex, but he has given scientists the insight needed to explore its rich details.

---

42. What is special about the North Star?

The most familiar star in the Northern Hemisphere is Polaris, the North Star. What is it that makes this star so well known? It is not the biggest star, nor the brightest, and certainly not the closest (its distance from Earth is 350 light-years, or 2,000 trillion miles away). What is unique about this star is that it does not appear to move. All of the other visible stars move across the night sky from east to west and also change positions with the seasons. However, since Polaris is situated almost directly above the earth's north pole, as the earth spins the star remains in a constant position in the northern sky. On a long time scale this alignment of Polaris with the earth's axis slowly changes. The earth's tilt remains the same, but its axis swings around in a circle (see figure 5). One complete turn takes about 26,000 years. This motion is called precession and is due to the gravity pull of the nearby moon. Back when the pyramids were being built, there was a different star above the earth's rotation axis. Passageways built into the pyramids were aligned with this previous polestar, called Thuban. During our lifetime, no movement of Polaris from its special position will be noticeable.

Polaris is an important star for navigation. From any location on the earth above the equator, the angle of Polaris above the horizon determines one's latitude. For example, if you are at a latitude of 41°, the polestar will be 41° above the northern horizon. Early explorers on land and sea carefully used sextants to measure the latitude of Polaris and thus determine their location. The sun can also be used, but the process is not as direct. Below the equator, Polaris is permanently out of sight. And no convenient star lies beyond the south pole to help find one's southern location, a serious concern to early explorers. Today, of course, navigation is aided by satellite communication.

Recent studies have shown that birds too, use the stars to navigate. During their annual migrations, many species of birds appear to orient their flights in the direction of various constellations.

Polaris is fairly bright and appears to stand by itself, high in the northern sky. To locate Polaris for yourself, the Big Dipper is useful. Two pointer stars in the "cup" of the Big Dipper lead the way to Polaris (figure 6). The polestar can also be seen at the end of the "handle" of the Little Dip-

Figure 5

Earth's precession
*The circle drawn above the earth shows the path
of the earth's axis as it slowly changes direction.*

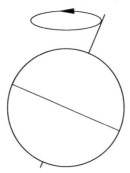

per, although this constellation is difficult to see because its member stars are quite dim.

What actually is this pinpoint of light called Polaris? Measurements show it to be a fiery sphere, 1,600 times brighter than our sun. The brightness of Polaris changes slightly from night to night since it is an unusual type of star that expands and contracts somewhat like a giant bubble. If the sun did this, the earth's temperature would fluctuate by hundreds of degrees each week. Changes in the weather would then really be a subject to talk about! Fortunately, the sun is a star with very steady light. Telescopes show a second, pale blue star that orbits Polaris, and there may be other unseen companions as well. The faraway polestar is a complex system that gives us only a

Figure 6

Locating Polaris

The outline of the Big Dipper constellation, also called Ursa Major.
The two end stars in the cup point the way toward Polaris.

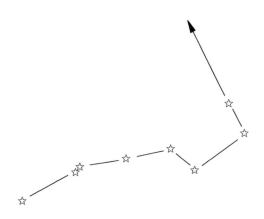

glimpse of its beauty and design. The vast energy and distance of Polaris are beyond understanding but not beyond appreciation.

---

43. Which is the brightest star?

The sun dominates our sky because it is the nearest star. However, there are distant stars that are actually much brighter than the sun. Consider Sirius, which appears to be the most brilliant evening star. This blue-white star is the fifth closest star to the earth at 8.8 light-years, or 1/2 million times the earth-sun distance. Sirius is also twice the size of our sun, and its high temperature produces the light of 23 suns. You can locate Sirius at the lower corner of a bright triangle of stars in the winter sky. The upper corners are formed by Procyon and Betelgeuse, stars in the constellations Canis Minor and Orion.

Sirius has had at least two other popular names. The ancient Egyptians called it the Nile Star, probably because it made an annual appearance in the morning sky in June, just before the rising of the Nile River. Sirius thus signaled the time of rejuvenation of farmland, and also marked Egypt's New Year. Others called Sirius the Dog Star, and it serves as the eye of Canis Major, a constellation shaped somewhat like a dog. Roman farmers around 238 B.C. practiced the pagan custom of sacrificing red-haired dogs to Sirius during their festivals. This was supposed to prevent rust and mildew in the fields, problems that were often attributed to Sirius in early astrology. More recently, some have thought that this bright star is responsible for the scorching "dog days" of late summer. Sirius is indeed present in the daytime sky during August, but is much too far away to supply any heat to the earth.

Sirius actually consists of a pair of stars. There is a small, faint *dwarf* star that orbits the larger and brighter star once each 50 years and is affectionately called the Pup. Just one handful of this dense dwarf star material would weigh ten tons! About 1,500 years ago, the dwarf star was most likely much larger than at present. It was then a red giant type of star (see Question 53), and eyewitnesses recorded that the entire Sirius system had a red appearance. As stars age, many may experience this shrinkage in size from giant to dwarf stages, with accompanying color changes. The changing Sirius star does not fit the pattern of those who believe in very long ages and slow changes of the stars, but the historical data cannot be denied. The Sirius star system demonstrates a rapidly changing universe and thus perhaps a much younger age than evolutionists theorize.

---

44. What are "wandering stars"?

In Jude 13 the title "wandering stars" is given to false teachers. These are leaders who lead people astray. In a similar way, a literal wandering star is one that is of no use for navigation since it does not keep its same relative position among the other stars. Such "restless" night lights were noticed in Bible times and are today known as planets, a word that comes from the Greek for "wanderer" as used in Jude 13. Since planets circle the sun, they appear to slowly move through the background stars from night to night. They spend some months in a particular constellation and then move on. Planets are not usually placed on standard star charts because such charts would soon become outdated and misleading. Planets may look much like stars, but they behave very differently. They are wanderers and are not dependable guide stars.

45. What was the Star of Bethlehem?

There have been many attempts to explain the Christmas Star scientifically, and three ideas will be mentioned here. Some scholars think this "star" was a comet, an object traditionally connected with important events in history, such as the birth of kings. However, records of comet sightings do not match up with the Lord's birth. For example, Halley's comet was present in 11 B.C., but the first Christmas took place around 5 to 7 B.C. Others believe that the Star of Bethlehem was a conjunction, or gathering of planets in the night sky. Since planets orbit the sun at different speeds and distances, they occasionally seem to approach each other closely. Johannes Kepler (1571–1630) preferred this view. However, multiple planets do not look like a single light source, as described in Scripture. Also, planet alignments are rather frequent and therefore not that unusual. There *was* a conjunction of Jupiter and Saturn in 6 B.C., but an even closer gathering in 66 B.C., much too early! Finally, an exploding star, or supernova, has been proposed to explain the Christmas Star. Some stars are unstable and explode in this way with a bright blaze. However, historical records do not indicate a supernova at the time of the Lord's birth (see Question 54).

All three explanations for the Star of Bethlehem fall short of the nativity story as predicted in Numbers 24:17 and recorded in Matthew 2:1–12. Two details in Matthew are of special interest. First, the text implies that only the Magi saw the star. However comets, conjunctions, and exploding stars would be visible to everyone on Earth. Second, the star went before the Magi and led them directly from Jerusalem to Bethlehem. This is a distance of about six miles, in a direction from north to south. However, every *natural* object in the sky moves from east to west due to the earth's rotation. It also is difficult to imagine how a natural light could lead the way to a particular house.

The conclusion is that the Star of Bethlehem cannot be naturally explained by science! It was a temporary and supernatural light. After all, the first Christmas was a time of miracles. God has often used special, heavenly lights to guide his people, such as the glory that filled the tabernacle (Exod. 40:34–38) and the temple (1 Kings 8:10) and that shone upon the apostle Paul (Acts 9:3). Such visible signs of God's presence are known as the Shekinah Glory, or dwelling place of God. This special light is a visible manifestation of divine majesty. The great mystery of the first Christmas is not the origin of its special star. It is the question of why the Magi were chosen to follow the light to the Messiah and why we are given the same invitation today.

---

46. What is the morning star?

"Morning star" is a name often used to describe the planet Venus. For part of each year Venus rises in the eastern sky, ahead of the sun. Since it is a very bright planet and remains visible into the morning hours, it is called a *morning* star even though it isn't really a star at all. During other parts of the year, Venus becomes an *evening* star. Then it sets in the west, after the sun. Whether visible in the morning or evening, Venus never moves very far from the sun because it is an inner planet. Mercury also qualifies as a morning and evening light, but it is more difficult to see.

In Scripture the title *morning star* is used in three different ways. First, Job 38:7 describes angels as morning stars (or day stars) that sang together at the creation of the universe. Angels were part of the initial creation (Col. 1:16)

73

and thus became witnesses of the great event. Second, the king of Babylon is described as a morning star and also a fallen star (Isa. 14:4, 12). This evil leader fell from the highest position to the lowest, just as Satan did. Third, the Lord Jesus is described as "the bright Morning Star" (Rev. 22:16), which rises in our hearts (2 Peter 1:19). Early morning stargazers often watch the eastern sky to see the brilliant planet Venus rise to signal a new day. As Christians—children of God—we are told to shine "like stars in the universe" (Phil. 2:15).

47. What are the Pleiades?

The beautiful group of stars known as the Pleiades is mentioned three times in Scripture. Job 9:8–9 and Amos 5:8 explain their origin, stating that the Creator "stretches out the heavens" and is the Maker of the Pleiades. Job 38:31–32 further declares that only the Lord can "bind the beautiful Pleiades" and bring them forth in their season. These stars are indeed gravitationally bound together in a cluster. They appear in the November skies and are located above Orion's left shoulder, where six icy-blue stars can be seen in the shape of a little dipper, smaller than the moon. Binoculars reveal dozens of additional stars in the Pleiades group, adding up to about 735 solar masses total. The stars are 380 light-years away but are actually near-neighbors of Earth in the Milky Way Galaxy.

The Pleiades stars have been described in many different ways. Chinese records from 2357 B.C. describe them as golden bees or flying pigeons. The Greeks named the stars the "Seven Sisters." Early Russian literature pictures the Pleiades as a mother hen with her chicks. For a while during the 1800s, it was thought that the Pleiades were located at the exact center of the universe since measurements seemed to show that all the other stars moved around the Pleiades. Today we know that the Pleiades star group itself also moves; it is actually speeding away from the earth continually at 16,000 miles per hour (see also Question 48).

48. What do we know about the stars named in Scripture?

Table 4 summarizes the stars and constellations that are mentioned in Scripture.

Pleiades. This small patch of icy-blue stars appears in the November sky. These stars are 380 light-years away and are near neighbors of the sun in the Milky Way Galaxy. As previously mentioned (Question 47), in the 1800s it was thought that the Pleiades star cluster was located at the exact center of the universe because measurements had shown that all other stars seemed to move around the Pleiades. Today we know that the Pleiades cluster itself also moves. We also know that the center of the universe has not been found! The Job 9 reference explains the origin of these stars, stating that the Creator stretches out the heavens and makes the Pleiades.

Bear and Cubs. The Big and Little Dippers are known as the Bear and her Cubs (Ursa Major and Ursa Minor). The bright component stars are located prominently in the northern sky. They are circumpolar stars that never set, as seen from northern latitudes. The King James Version of Scripture translates the Hebrew name as Arcturus, another possible identification. The star called Arcturus is positioned today in the summer constellation Bootes, some distance from the dipper stars.

Orion. The Hunter constellation dominates the winter sky each year. Since it is positioned directly above the earth's equator, Orion is easily seen by people everywhere on the earth. Its two main stars, Rigel and Betelgeuse, are the seventh and twelfth brightest stars in the entire night sky. The Job 38 reference declares that God alone can hold together the stars of the Pleiades and Orion constellations.

Castor and Pollux. Part of the Gemini constellation, in ancient times these two stars were thought to be guardians of sailors. In Roman mythology, Castor was a horse trainer and his twin brother, Pollux, a boxer. On Paul's journey to Rome, his ship sailed under the figurehead of Castor and Pollux (Acts 28:11).

Table 4
Stars and Constellations in Scripture

	Job 9:9	Job 38:31–32	Amos 5:8	Acts 28:11
Pleiades	*	*	*	
Bear and her Cubs	*	*		
Orion	*	*	*	
Castor and Pollux				*

49. Is the gospel spelled out in the stars?

It has long been suggested that the constellations are God-given illustrations of gospel truths. Indeed, constellation names go far back into mankind's history. The Jewish historian Josephus says they were named by Seth, the third son of Adam, but perhaps even Adam had a part, since he named the animal world (Gen. 2:19). The Bible says that God assigns his own names to the stars (Ps. 147:4). If so, he may have revealed them to early people.

Of special interest are the twelve zodiac constellations. This band of stars lies in the plane of the solar system.

They appear high in the night sky, roughly along the same path traveled by the sun during the day. During the course of each year the zodiac constellations take turns in appearing: for example, Scorpius in summer, Gemini in winter. Job 38:32 makes reference to the bringing forth of these constellations (or "Mazzaroth" in KJV) in their season.

The idea of seeing the gospel message in the stars was popularized by the writings of E. W. Bullinger and J. A. Seiss during the 1800s. According to this theory, table 5 is a brief outline of the usual zodiac interpretations.

Table 5
Zodiac Interpretations

Constellation	Picture	Interpretation
Virgo	Virgin	Virgin Mary
Libra	Scales	Sin must be paid for
Scorpius	Scorpion	Sin brings death
Sagittarius	Archer	Demonism
Capricorn	Goat-fish	Earth Corruption
Aquarius	Water pourer	Living water or Noah's flood
Pisces	Fish	God's remnant
Aries	Ram	Sacrifice
Taurus	Bull	Resurrection
Gemini	Twins	Christ's dual nature
Cancer	Crab	Gathering of redeemed
Leo	Lion	The King

Early writings on this subject went into great detail regarding different parts of the constellations, so that practically every star was assigned a special meaning. The gospel message may well have been purposely written in the skies by the Lord. In that case, perhaps the star signs served as memory aids before Scripture was available. Today, of course, the Bible provides a clear message about the plan of God. Although stars continue to "declare the glory of God" (Ps. 19:1) and are useful in our calendar system (Gen. 1:14), the Bible does not tell us to search the stars for detailed messages. On the contrary, warnings are given against trusting in the stars. Caution is needed when searching for the gospel in the stars, since constellation symbols can have many possible interpretations. Since Babylonian times, Satan has counterfeited the zodiac with astrology.

Many people still claim to see symbols of the gospel in unusual places: crosses on flower petals, Christmas stars on sand dollars, or even religious images on rusty water towers! God certainly designed all things, but we must beware of building our doctrines on the details of nature. We can be thankful that the Bible presents the gospel to us so clearly that we have no need for additional evidence of its truths.

50. Did the stars fight against Sisera?

Judges 4 tells of the defeat of Sisera, a Canaanite military leader who fought against Israel, the Lord's chosen people. In the end he lost his entire army as well as his own life. Judges 5 is the victorious song of Deborah, the prophetess who led Israel at this time, and verse 20 declares that the battle with Sisera was a heavenly one: "From the heavens the stars fought, from their courses they fought against Sisera." This is a poetic way of saying that the powers of heaven fought on Israel's behalf. The Lord and his host of angels assured the defeat of the Canaanites. Those who oppose God's plans have no more chance of success than if they opposed the motion of the stars above.

51. What is a black hole?

Black holes are invisible, weigh billions of tons, and are smaller than a kernel of corn! They have been made popular by science-fiction movies and video games, but black holes were first postulated by the French astronomer Pierre Laplace more than 200 years ago. He realized that stars must collapse when they run short of fuel. If a star is heavy enough, there should be no limit to its contraction. It will first shrink to the size of the moon, then the size of a basketball. Finally it will have no size at all, as gravity crushes the entire star down to a mathematical point. The only meaningful size reference is a spherical "event horizon" around the collapsed star. The size of this sphere depends on the mass of the original star and may extend outward for millions of miles. Anything entering this region could not possibly withstand the inward gravity pull of the collapsed star. Even light cannot escape, hence the name "black hole."

Although black holes cannot be seen directly, there are ways to detect them in space since they should affect nearby stars, possibly tearing them apart and producing x-rays in the process. One likely location for a black hole is in the constellation Cygnus (the Swan), also known as the Northern Cross. The suspected region is called Cygnus X–1, a strong source of x-ray radiation. These x-rays do not harm us on Earth but are readily measured by satellites. Cygnus X–1 may be a black hole—or it may be some other unusual type of star.

Other evidence points to massive black holes in the center of many galaxies. However, except in movies, no black holes have yet been positively identified. Some recent theories in physics conclude that "black hole" stars are not stable. If this is true, they may eventually evaporate into other kinds of matter. For the Christian, it doesn't really matter since—if black holes indeed exist—they are evidence for the decay of the universe. A black hole is, after all, a collapsed star, yet another phenomenon that illustrates the unending variety of created objects in the sky.

Some Christians have speculated that black holes might be God's energy reservoirs, needed for the future formation of the "new heaven and new earth." Black holes certainly contain vast energy, as does every star. However, energy reservoirs are hardly needed by the One who spoke the universe into being by the power of his word.

---

52. What is the Death Star?

Some scientists speculate that the sun has an unseen companion star whose orbit brings it close to the solar system about once every 26 million years. On each trip inward, this star unleashes numerous comets from the Oort cloud (see Question 28). According to this theory, on a previous pass (about 65 million years ago), many of these comets struck the earth. This resulted in explosive collisions that pushed a great dark cloud of dust into the upper atmosphere and thus shielded the earth's surface from sunlight for many years. Since plants could not grow, the vegetarian dinosaurs starved, and the broken food chain soon affected the carnivorous animals as well. Geologists call this the Cretaceous extinction (see Question 29).

The star that supposedly started all this is appropriately named Nemesis—the Death Star—after the Greek goddess of punishment. The search for this disturbing star has been unsuccessful. Perhaps the reason is that the star does not exist! Creationists have a more credible explanation for the period of widespread destruction, based on the Genesis flood. It is interesting to note that the disappearance of the dinosaurs has forced scientists to postulate many worldwide catastrophes. They have abandoned James Hutton's "uniformitarianism," whereby all changes on Earth are slow, and the present is the key to the past. The creationist position has always emphasized the role of biblical catastrophes in earth history.

---

53. Which are the largest stars?

There are indeed some giants in the sky! The largest stars are called *red giants* or super-giants. Their diameters reach more than 500 times that of our sun. If such a super-giant star could be positioned at the center of the solar system, the four inner planets, including the earth, would be vaporized beneath the star's surface. These giant stars generally have a red appearance due to their relatively "cool" surface temperature, around 5000° F. Some of the well-known red giants, in order of increasing size, are:

Arcturus is a yellow-red star, the fourth brightest in the sky. It is 20 times larger than the sun. Arcturus is sometimes called Job's star, due to its possible mention in Job 9:9 and 38:32. As a publicity stunt, light from Arcturus was used to trigger the opening of the Chicago "Century of Progress" Exposition in 1933. As the star moved in front of a carefully placed telescope, it triggered a light-sensitive switch. Arcturus was chosen because it was thought to be 40 light-years away, so its light had actually left the star at the time of a previous fair in Chicago, in 1893. More recently the distance to Arcturus has been measured at 36 light-years.

Aldebaran is the eye of Taurus (the Bull). Red giants make bright eyes for constellations! Aldebaran is about 70 light-years away, and is 45 solar diameters in size. This bright star is occasionally covered up, or occulted, by the moon.

Antares is an orange-red star, the eye of the Scorpion constellation. The name means "rival of Mars," which describes the star's planetlike appearance. Antares has a diameter that is 700 times the size of the sun and shines with the brightness of 9,000 suns.

Betelgeuse is the right shoulder of Orion (the Hunter). The diameter of this giant star is 1,200 times that of the sun. Betelgeuse also gives off 120,000 times as much light energy as the sun.

---

54. What is a supernova?

Certain large stars may undergo a sudden explosion called a supernova event. Stars are thought to be heated by the nuclear fusion of hydrogen into helium. More massive stars continue this fusion process by combining the heavier elements. Their stellar cores fuse helium into carbon, then oxygen, and continue upward to the element iron. However, iron atoms will not undergo fusion to still heavier elements. With the nuclear energy process extinguished at this point, gravity then causes the star to collapse upon itself. This sudden contraction heats the star greatly and triggers a destructive explosion. In just hours the disintegrating star may increase its brightness to that of a billion suns, and star debris is ejected outward at thousands of miles per second. As the light fades over the following months, a *nebula* cloud of dust and gas is left behind to mark the event. This cloud may gradually grow to trillions of miles in size. The supernova may also leave behind the core of the original star in the midst of the cloud. This compact residue is a rapidly spinning *neutron star*, also called a *pulsar.* Some of these highly magnetized, compact pulsars rotate hundreds of times each second.

Little is actually known about the internal behavior of stars. Therefore the previous description is speculative. Models predict that a star with at least three times the mass of the sun may become a supernova as described. The process marks the wearing out and death of large stars. Thankfully our sun lacks sufficient mass to self-destruct in this manner. Supernovas are yet another reminder that the physical universe is temporary and sometimes violent in nature.

One famous supernova was observed by Chinese astronomers in 1054 A.D. The star explosion was as bright as Venus in the night sky, and for several months could be seen even during the day. The Crab Nebula remains today at the site of this historic space explosion. A supernova explosion is a rare event. The last one in the Milky Way was recorded by astronomers Kepler and Galileo in 1604, four centuries ago. In 1987 a more distant supernova made headlines when it was observed in the Large Magellanic Cloud, a neighboring galaxy that lies 180,000 light-years away.

---

55. Do stars evolve?

Some of what astronomers describe as "stellar evolution" does take place. However, the process is misnamed, and parts of it are questionable. According to this theory, the life of a star is said to begin with the collapse of a gas cloud—a doubtful beginning, as explained in Question 56. Bypassing this fundamental origin problem, a young star is said to begin in the "main-sequence" category (see Question 98). These are average stars with a stable light output. The great majority of stars are in the main sequence, including our sun. Then when a star's hydrogen fuel runs low, it becomes a *red giant* or super-giant star. The star expands hundreds of times in size and becomes somewhat cooler. Red giants include Betelgeuse and Aldebaran. Next, the star may either explode as a *supernova* or may slowly collapse into a small, hot *white dwarf* star. The companion star circling Sirius is such a dwarf (see Question 43). Such stars are said to be very old.

Notice that the entire life of a star is an aging process: main sequence—red giant—white dwarf. Instead of stellar evolution, it might better be called stellar decay, degradation, or degeneration. Computer studies conclude that each stage of a star lasts for millions or billions of years (depending on the star's mass), but—in the recent-creation view—there has not been enough time for such change. And some observed star changes appear to be much more rapid than computer models suggest! For example, there is evidence that the dwarf companion of Sirius formed from a red giant in just 1,000 years. Other stars have also shown unexpected color changes, indicating that the aging process of some stars may be much more rapid than generally believed. Most stars have probably not changed substantially in appearance since the creation described in Genesis. They were probably made in all their variety, much as we see them today, including dwarfs and giants. The sun has certainly remained as a faithful "main sequence" star from the beginning. Since all the stars were made on the fourth day (Gen. 1:16–19), they are all actually the same age. From the beginning they have differed from each other in color and brightness—"in splendor" (1 Cor. 15:41).

56. Do new stars form today?

The complete birth of a star has never been observed. The principles of physics demand some special conditions for star formation and also a long time period. A cloud of hydrogen gas must be compressed to a sufficiently small size so that gravity dominates. (As an example, the sun is a stable sphere of gas.) In space, however, almost every gas cloud is light-years in size, hundreds of times greater than the critical size needed for a stable star. As a result, outward gas pressures cause these clouds to spread out farther, not contract.

A number of mechanisms have been proposed to trigger the beginning of star formation. Most popular is a pressure or density wave in space, which might squeeze dust clouds down to star-forming size. This pressure wave is suggested to originate from a nearby supernova or exploding star. The net result is that stars are said to form from other stars. But where do the first stars come from in this circular reasoning? Another problem for this theory of stellar origins is the great distance between stars. Most are isolated from each other by ten light-years or more and thus would appear unable to influence each other's origin in any significant way.

Scientists point to certain areas where they believe stars may be forming today. One of these rare spots is the Orion Nebula, a glowing gas cloud in the December sky. The infrared radiation emitted from this cloud is thought to be perhaps related to the start-up energy from new stars. However, there is too much gas and dust to see these stars, and the source of this infrared radiation may actually be some type of star that has existed in the gas cloud for a long time. All assumptions regarding present-day star formation remain speculative.

The creationist also sees a time-scale problem with theories about present-day star formation. Although computer models typically give a million-year start-up time for new stars, such unlimited time is not available in a "young" universe. Observations of space reveal the universal trend of star degeneration, not star formation. Star formation *may* occur today in certain locations where conditions are met. However, it is doubtful that such rare star births can replace the many dying stars. Star decay is a fairly common event in the form of novas and supernovas. We can conclude that the universe of *created* stars is slowly aging.

57. Are we made of stardust?

This is the rather simplistic conclusion of the big bang theory (see Question 64), whereby the original chemical elements of the early universe are thought to be limited to hydrogen, helium, and lithium. According to this secular view, all the other elements, now numbering 111, were later formed by nuclear reactions within the cores of ancient stars. When these stars eventually exploded as supernovae, their many elements were spread far and wide throughout space. The solar system, including the life upon planet Earth, is thought to be made of this star debris. Thus has arisen the poetic generalization that we are all "made of stardust" or star debris and are therefore "one with the universe." This false idea fits in well with the New Age movement, which sees mystical connections between humanity and nature. Man—in the form of Adam—was indeed made from the "dust" of the ground. However, the earth and its component materials were created *before* the stars, not *from* the stars (Gen. 1:16).

58. What are the southern skies like?

The earth maintains a permanent tilt of its north-south axis as it circles the sun. The angle of this tilt is 23.5°, as can be seen on any classroom globe. As a result, we in the Northern Hemisphere never get a look at the stars in the far southern skies. Likewise, the North Star cannot be seen by people below the equator. Notable stars in the Southern Hemisphere include Alpha Centauri, the earth's nearest star after the sun, and Canopus, the second brightest star after Sirius. The Southern Cross, which is the smallest constellation in the sky, lies close to the southern celestial pole. Countries "down under" are proud of this small but bright constellation, and the Southern Cross can be found on several national flags. It is interesting that distinct cross constellations are present in both the northern and southern skies: the Swan, or Northern Cross, in the north, and the Southern Cross (Crux) in the south. Two fuzzy patches of light are also seen in the southern sky. They mark galaxies of stars called the Magellanic Clouds. These are our nearest visible galaxies and are about 180,000 light-years away. Wherever one travels on planet Earth, the land is filled with God's goodness and the skies are filled with his glory!

---

59. Does everyone see the same stars?

From the perspective of the Northern Hemisphere, everyone sees roughly the same stars on a given night. If it is December, the same winter stars are seen from both North America and from Europe, but one's latitude will determine how high a given star appears in the sky. From the Southern Hemisphere, stars in the far north, such as Polaris and the Big Dipper constellation, remain hidden below the horizon. These are replaced by such southern stars as Alpha Centauri and the Southern Cross, which cannot be seen from the northern latitudes.

60. Did a vapor canopy once hide the stars?

The term *vapor canopy* refers to a reservoir of moisture that may have existed in the upper atmosphere from the time of creation until the Genesis flood. Possible biblical references include the separation of waters above and below the "firmament" (Gen. 1:6–7) and the opening of the "floodgates" of heaven (Gen. 7:11). The canopy is thought to have collapsed at the time of the flood, so there is no direct way to verify its earlier existence. The vapor canopy remains as an optional part of the creation model. Such a canopy would probably not have been visible. We know that water in the form of gaseous vapor (isolated molecules) is invisible, and that there is always unseen moisture (humidity) present in the air. Water in the atmosphere becomes visible only when a million or more water molecules join together as fog or cloud droplets. The white "vapor trails" that sometimes appear behind jet airplanes are not really gaseous vapor at all but water drops that form from the aircraft fuel or from the air. When the drops vaporize or dissipate, the "contrail" disappears.

Since, in large quantities, water vapor will absorb and scatter light, the earth's vapor canopy may have somewhat dimmed the heavenly lights. One technical study concluded that a canopy-covered night sky might have looked the same as a night when a full moon is present. If this is correct, the dim stars may have remained unseen. However, the canopy would certainly not have hidden the sun, moon, or brightest stars. We know from Scripture that from the very beginning, the heavens have served their purpose as lights for the earth, markers for seasons, and reminders of God's great glory.

61. How can we see distant stars in a "young" universe?

This is a frequently asked question in Creation Science. If the universe is only about 10,000 years old, how can we see galaxies that are millions or billions of light-years away? Many suggestions have been offered, and some follow, with pertinent comments.

1. *Stars are nearby.* This view holds that all the stars are actually quite close to us, within a few thousand light-years. However, the universe must be much larger than this to hold the vast number of stars we see. The Milky Way Galaxy with its 100 billion stars is 100,000 light-years across. And uncounted other galaxies can be seen as dim, distant islands in space. The only alternative to vast size is that these galaxies are some kind of miniature lights nearby. But this is implausible and also opposes the glory evident in the heavens. The "nearby star" view must be rejected.

2. *Space is curved.* It is suggested that distant starlight reaches us quickly by taking a "shortcut" along some kind of curved path through space. Curved space is a mathematical concept that is difficult to visualize. Also, the observed distribution of stars in space does not seem to support this idea. It must be realized, however, that we know very little about the geometry of deep space. Almost any mathematical arrangement could be suggested.

3. *Decaying light speed.* If the speed of light was greater in the past, early starlight could have moved more rapidly across space than today. This idea is fully described in Question 97.

4. *Relativistic cosmology.* Relativity theory is involved in this question. Time itself appears to be somewhat variable

in duration for an object that experiences extremes of gravity or speed. In this way separate time frames may exist at various locations, depending on local conditions. While only a short time passes on Earth, there may be adequate longer time in space for faraway starlight to reach us.

5. *Mature Creation.* The dispersed light was created together with the stars and instantly spread out across space. This fifth solution is simple and is entirely consistent with the creation account. The Garden of Eden was formed with trees already bearing fruit, and Adam and Eve were created as adults. Similarly, we can conclude that the universe was formed as a fully functioning whole, not in an infant stage. Consider the alternative: Since the nearest star, Alpha Centauri, is about four light-years away, Adam and Eve would not have seen even this star for the first four years. Then the stars would have slowly blinked on, one by one. Yet, the Bible tells us that from the beginning, stars have had the purpose of providing a calendar system (Gen. 1:14). Therefore they must have been visible from the moment of their creation on the fourth day. In our own day, we do not see new stars "turning on" in the night sky, as if their light finally is reaching the earth. Instead, this option states that starlight was created as part of each star and was present throughout space from the beginning of time.

In the *last days*, there will be rapid, dramatic changes in the sky (see Question 87). According to Isaiah 34:4, the heavens will be rolled up like a scroll. However, these heavens extend outward for billions of light-years. If the future heavens can be instantly altered in this way, then surely they also could have been created instantly with a mature appearance.

PART FOUR

Galaxies
and the Universe

---

62. What is the Milky Way?

Our galaxy, the Milky Way, can be seen in all its glory on clear, moonless nights. Appearing as a diffuse band of glowing light, it stretches across the sky roughly from north to south. The path of soft light looks like a trail of clouds or smoke (except that it doesn't blow away), and the farther you are from city lights, the more majestic it becomes. In mythology, the Milky Way was known as a heavenly river that led to the world beyond. American Indians looked at the many bright stars that shine beside this "river" in the sky and pictured them as the campfires of departed warriors.

Galileo, in 1610, was the first astronomer to view the Milky Way in detail with a telescope. Instead of a fabled celestial river, the glowing band was seen to be made up of countless, distant stars. The telescope also showed that the heavens were far larger than previously thought. The Milky Way is actually a pancake-shaped cluster of stars.

Figure 7
The Milky Way Galaxy
The top view is above and the edge view below.
The galaxy's diameter is 100,000 light years.
The small dots represent stars; the large dot shows
the location of the sun and earth.

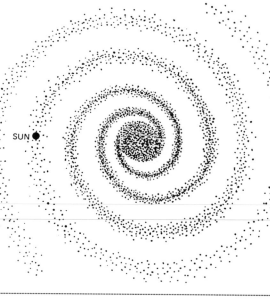

There is a bulge in the center where the "batter" of stars is extra thick (see figure 7).

The outer regions of our galaxy are thought to have the shape of spiral arms. The details are uncertain, simply because we live *inside* the Milky Way and cannot get a look at our galaxy from the outside. The best information comes by looking beyond the Milky Way toward other galaxies.

Then we see the delicate pinwheel shape of these other vast islands of stars.

The Milky Way consists of 100 billion stars. If divided up, there would be dozens of Milky Way stars for every person on Earth! If one could travel across the span of our galaxy at the speed of light, the time required would be 100,000 years. The distance traveled would be about 600,000 trillion miles. Such numbers quickly become even more incomprehensible than the federal debt!

The earth is located about two-thirds of the way out toward the edge of the Milky Way. Instead of living in the bright central hub, we are in a spiral arm, "out in the countryside" of the galaxy. To visualize this, consider a penny as a model of the Milky Way. Planet Earth would then be placed within a single number in the date. Also inside the small number would be the other planets, the sun, and all the stars we can see. The visible stars of the night sky are all very close to us. Distance and obscuring dust prevent us from seeing the remaining 99 percent of the Milky Way Galaxy. Here is another illustration of size: If the solar system was as small as a coffee cup, the Milky Way would be the size of North America!

Far beyond the Milky Way, other galaxies of stars seem to extend forever. Astronomers have named a few of them: Andromeda, Magellanic Clouds, and the Whirlpool Galaxy. There is even a galaxy called Snickers! The grand total of the multitude of stars in all the galaxies is immense. The number closely matches estimates of the grains of sand on all the seashores (see Questions 39, 91). And every star is similar to the sun, a vast reservoir of heat and light. The study of galaxies certainly teaches us a lesson in mankind's smallness and God's glory.

63. Is the universe expanding?

Measurements indicate that the universe is continually expanding, or spreading out. Current belief is that space itself is enlarging, carrying along the galaxies that are embedded within space. The most distant galaxies and quasars seem to have departing speeds that are close to the speed of light. The evidence is based on the redshift of light. If a light source such as a galaxy is moving away from the earth, there will be a shift toward the longer wavelength end of the spectrum, that is, in the direction of red-colored light. This shift is noticed for nearly all of the galaxies beyond those in the vicinity of the Milky Way. Such galaxies don't actually turn red, but their spectra reveal the shift of their wavelength toward longer wavelengths.

The redshift of starlight is often taken as evidence for the big bang theory (see next two questions). Yesterday the universe was a bit smaller than it is today, and it was smaller yet a year ago. By this backward extrapolation, the universe is hypothetically contracted to a single point of explosion some 10 to 15 billion years ago. It must be noted that extrapolation can be a dangerous practice in science, for two particular reasons in this case. First, a guess must be made concerning rates of change in the past. When God placed the stars in the sky, there was *instant* expansion! Therefore, present rates of change should *not* be used to try to interpret the distant past. Second, extrapolation may not be taken beyond the actual beginning point. If the universe is 10,000 years old, that must be the limit of extrapolation. Expansion of the universe is just one possible explanation for the redshift of starlight (see Question 66). If this theory is correct, God surely has his own purposes for creating a universe in outward motion. Perhaps it provides stability: In a static universe, gravity would cause all galaxies to eventually collapse inward.

64. What is the big bang theory?

The "big bang" is a popular, secular explanation for the origin of the universe. The theory will be outlined here without commenting on its problems and deficiencies (see next question). The process began with the explosion of a nugget, or "kernel," of mass energy about 15 billion years ago. As the energetic radiation spread outward, temperatures slowly cooled enough for hydrogen and helium atoms to form. Some time later, the first stars began to form from the cooling gas in the young universe. This star-forming process eventually gave rise to the Milky Way Galaxy. When these initial stars had sufficiently aged, some of them became supernovae explosions. The resulting star fragments later recombined into new stars to repeat the formation-disintegration process. Our sun is said to be a third-generation star, a relatively recent addition to the family of stars, and to have formed around 5 billion years ago. Other star fragments are thought to have provided the raw material for planets and people. Figure 8 is a brief summary of the big bang theory.

Figure 8

Big Bang Theory

An outline of supposed events, from initial explosion to the origin of the solar system.

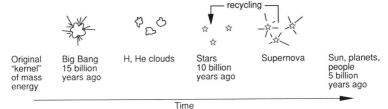

| Original "kernel" of mass energy | Big Bang 15 billion years ago | H, He clouds | Stars 10 billion years ago | Supernova | Sun, planets, people 5 billion years ago |

Time

One modification of this story is called the oscillating big bang theory. This is an attempt to avoid having to explain the initial event. Any unexplained origin is embarrassing to science, even if it is only an explosion! According to this theory, the universe ceases to expand after a while and begins to fall back on itself. Gravity then pulls everything in toward the original kernel of mass energy. Any record of the prior universe is eventually burned and destroyed completely. The kernel then reexplodes outward and a new universe begins. The time period between the "big bangs" is estimated at 40 billion years. The theory of a self-generating, oscillating universe is similar to ancient Greek ideas of eternal cycles. It is convenient to secular thinking because an oscillating universe is thought to avoid both a definitive origin and a final destiny for all matter, both living and nonliving.

65. *Was* there a big bang?

The big bang is usually defined as a random, chance event. As noted in the previous question, some instability supposedly developed in an original "kernel" of mass energy, and the universe then ballooned outward. However, Scripture clearly rules out such an accidental origin. A modified view of the big bang theory says that when the explosive event happened, it was directed by God. This is called theistic evolution and is an attempt to compromise the Bible with long-age evolutionary theories. It is rejected by many creationists because of its conflicts with the order of events in Genesis. Table 6 contrasts some of the chronological discrepancies between the Bible's creation account and the big bang theory.

Table 6
Chronological Discrepancies between Scripture and the Big Bang

Scripture	Big Bang
All elements made together	Elements beyond hydrogen and helium formed after millions of years
Earth formed before stars	Earth formed long after the stars
Plants formed before the sun	Plants evolved after the sun
Birds created before reptiles, mammals	Birds evolved from reptiles
Sun formed on the fourth day, after the earth	Sun formed before the earth
Sun, moon, and stars formed together	Sun formed from older stars

Creationists maintain that in the beginning God spoke and the earth appeared—he commanded and the heavens stood firm (Ps. 33:9)! All the many stars appeared suddenly and supernaturally in space. Scripture does not imply an explosion, although the universe must have experienced a sudden, "explosive" input of ordered energy. Perhaps some astronomical data that seems supportive of the big bang theory, such as redshift and background radiation, needs to be looked at instead as evidence of a rapid creation. One secular variation of the big bang theory refers to an "inflationary" big bang, the suggestion being that the universe developed and matured very quickly in its first moments. In this particular theory, secular science seems to have taken one step in the creationist direction. Further developments should be of interest in this area of theory and research.

The big bang as it is understood today is an inadequate theory. There are many fundamental problems that are seldom mentioned in popular literature. Some of the "missing links" in the theory are:

Missing Origin. The big bang theory assumes an original concentration of energy. Where did this energy come from? Astronomers sometimes speak of an origin from a "quantum mechanical fluctuation within a vacuum." However, in the big bang theory, no vacuum existed before the explosion. Actually there is *no* consistent secular origin theory, since every idea is based on preexisting matter or energy.

Missing Fuse. What ignited the big bang? The mass concentration proposed in this theory would remain forever bound as a universal black hole. Gravity would prevent it from ever expanding outward.

Missing Star Formation. No natural way has been found to explain the formation of planets, stars, and galaxies. An explosion should produce, at best, an outward spray of gas and radiation. This gas should continue expanding, not form intricate planets, stars, and entire galaxies.

Missing Antimatter. Some versions of the big bang theory require the equal production of matter and antimatter. However, only small traces of antimatter—positrons and antiprotons, for example—are found in space.

Missing Time. Some experiments indicate that the universe may be young, on the order of 10,000 years old. If true, then there is not sufficient time for the consequences of the big bang theory to unfold. A short time span will not allow for the *gradual* evolution of the stars or life on Earth.

Missing Mass. Many scientists assume that the universe will eventually stop expanding and begin to collapse inward. Then it will again explode and repeat its oscillating type of perpetual motion. This idea is an effort to avoid an origin and destiny for the universe. For oscillation to occur, however, the universe must have a certain density or distribution of mass. So far, measurements of the mass density are 100 times smaller than expected. In fact there are indications that the universe is *accelerating* outward instead of slowing down. The universe does not appear to be oscillating. The necessary mass or "dark matter" is "missing."

Missing Life. In an evolving universe, life should have developed everywhere. Space should be filled with radio signals from intelligent life forms. Where is everybody?

Missing Neutrinos. These small particles should flood the earth from the sun's fusion process. The small number detected raises questions about the sun's energy source and man's overall understanding of the universe (see Question 31). How then can science speak about "origins" with any authority?

---

66. How is redshift explained?

The redshift of starlight is a decrease in the energy of the light. This energy decrease results in a lengthening of the wavelength of the light, measured with an instrument called a spectrometer. Red is the rainbow color with the longest wavelength, hence the name "redshift." Stars do not actually become red in appearance since the wavelength change is usually slight. Almost every star and galaxy beyond the Milky Way is found to be redshifted. Following are summaries of some of the alternative explanations for the origin of this stellar redshift.

Stellar Motion. If a star moves outward from the earth, its light energy will be reduced and its wavelength stretched or redshifted. The usual interpretation is that space itself is expanding. Stars and entire galaxies show varying amounts of redshift, therefore implying a variety of speeds for these objects. Police actually use this same effect with radar to measure the speed of cars. Stellar motion is often taken as evidence in support of the big bang theory. Stars are assumed to be speeding outward as a result of the explosion. This is not the only explanation for redshift, however.

Gravitation. As light leaves a star, the star's gravity may slightly lengthen the wavelength of the light. A gravitational redshift will also result from starlight passing near a massive object in space, such as a galaxy. As the light escapes from a strong gravity field, it loses energy, much like what happens to a person struggling to the top of a hill.

Second-Order Doppler Effect. A light source moving at right angles (tangentially) to an observer will always be redshifted. This can be observed in the laboratory by using a high-speed turntable. A detector is placed in the center and a gamma radiation source is placed on the outside edge. The gamma energy is seen to decrease, or "redshift," as the turntable speed increases. This is an intriguing explanation for stellar redshift. When applied to stars, it implies that the entire universe may be in circular motion instead of radial expansion.

Photon Interaction. It is possible that light waves exchange energy during their movement across space and lose some energy in the process. A loss of light energy is equivalent to a "reddening" of its light. A theoretical understanding of this proposed "tired light" process has not yet been developed.

Any of these four explanations, alone or in combination, may be responsible for redshift. We do not know enough about deep space to be certain of the source of stellar redshift.

---

67. What is background radiation?

Background radiation, a low-energy form of microwaves that permeates space, was first detected in 1965 by researchers at Bell Laboratories. The radiation has an energy that is equivalent to a temperature of 2.7 Kelvins, –270° C, or –455° F, just slightly above absolute zero. This can be considered the overall temperature of space. Background radiation has been made an integral part of the big bang theory. It is said that this low energy is the "last dying ember" from the original explosion and that—after 8 to 15 billion years—the universe has cooled down to this low temperature.

The redshift of starlight and this background radiation have become identified as the main evidence for the big bang. Largely because of the hypothesized significance of the radiation, its discoverers received a Nobel prize in physics in 1970. The Cosmic Background Explorer (COBE) satellite further explored this radiation in 1990. Slight deviations in the temperature of space were measured. This data is taken as evidence of concentrations of matter in the early universe, when galaxies first began to evolve. For the creationist who rejects the big bang theory, there are alternative explanations for the background radiation. It may result from the supernatural creation event itself. Or the radiation may be emitted from certain types of stars or galaxies, or from an unknown source. After all, space is also filled with cosmic rays, the source of which is not known with certainty.

---

68. Why does everything in space display circular motion?

God has created a dynamic universe in which the contents are in constant motion. *Rotation* is the turning of an object on its axis (like the spinning Earth), whereas *revolution* refers to the orbital motion of moons around planets and planets around the sun. Table 7 shows the rotation times for various objects in space. Several items in the list deserve additional comment. *Pulsars* are a category of collapsed stars that spin wildly. Their rotation is observed to slow down very gradually as energy is lost into space. As for the *earth,* rotation provides the obvious day/night cycle. The rotation time of *Comet Halley* was determined during its 1986 appearance. The sun, a gaseous sphere, turns faster at its equator than at the poles. The large rotation time for the Milky Way Galaxy does not mean that it is ancient. In the recent-creation view, this galaxy is still in its first rotation. The galaxy spin rate is not as lazy as it sounds; the entire solar system moves at 500,000 miles per hour around the galaxy. One purpose of the circular motion of all objects in space is to provide stability. If planets and moons did not have orbital motion, gravity would cause them to crash inward. If the Milky Way was a stationary group of stars, then the stars would also begin moving toward the center. The galaxy's rotation prevents this unstable situation.

Table 7
Rotation Periods for Objects in Space

Object	Rotational Period
Pulsar stars	.001–1 second
Jupiter	10 hours
Earth	24 hours
Comet Halley	48–168 hours
Moon	29 1/2 days
Sun	28 days (average)
Venus	243 days
Milky Way	225 million years

69. How old is the universe?

There are many measurements that purportedly give ages for the earth, moon, and stars, but one finds a wide range of estimates, depending on the assumptions made. At one extreme, details such as the influx of minerals into the oceans and the stability of Saturn's rings give a maximum age for the universe of only thousands of years. At the other extreme, radiometric dating of rocks seems to indicate billions of years. One can choose just about any age by selecting a particular experiment or basis of measurement. Even a single experiment can seemingly yield conflicting results, depending on the interpretation of the data. Creationists have emphasized the recent-age measurements, providing a much needed balance to the age issue. Many creationists believe that measurements indicating a "young universe" are much closer to the truth and that extreme-age results need critical scrutiny. Given the wide range of suggested age values, it appears unlikely that scientists will be able to settle the issue. There are too many variables, unknowns, and biases for there to be agreement on the age of anything as complex as the universe.

Scripture provides an alternative to the scientific debate over the age of the earth and universe beyond. The Bible is not ambiguous. It promotes a universal age between 6,000 and 10,000 years, the length of time that provides a sufficient framework for biblical history. In contrast, the current secular view regarding the age of the universe is 8 to 15 billion years, a time span that is a million times *longer* than the Bible indicates.

To force a long time scale on the universe is wrong for at least three reasons. First, it selects just one age view, admittedly the most popular one, from the many choices available in science. Second, the figure of 8 to 15 billion years is probably only temporary. As new dating techniques are perfected, the extreme-age scientists may change their estimated time scale of history to 15 thousand years or even to 15 trillion years. And where does this open-ended question leave the *unchanging* Scripture? Third, the secular view of science conflicts with Scripture in many details, the most important of which include creation versus evolution and purpose versus randomness in the universe.

---

70. What is a quasar?

Quasars are mysterious sources of distant light. The name stands for "quasi-stellar" objects. Since their discovery in 1962, hundreds of quasars have been detected with telescopes. They have been variously identified as exotic stars, colliding galaxies, and even black hole collisions. Many quasars appear to be associated with the cores of energetic galaxies. The main distinction of quasars is an extremely large redshift of their light. This would seem to imply an outward motion of the quasars at very high speeds. They are thought to be the most distant objects we have observed (perhaps 15 billion light-years away). Quasars must be very bright objects to be seen at such great distances. They appear to shine with the brilliance of entire galaxies, yet are millions of times smaller. They may be powered by material drawn by gravity into massive black holes within the quasars.

---

71. Is heaven located in the northern sky?

This recurring idea has apparent support from Job 26:7: "He [God] spreads out the northern skies over empty space." Although some Bible students have taken this verse to indicate a significant direction in space, perhaps the location of heaven, the reference more likely refers to the broad northern expanse in general. This particular direction may have been emphasized because of the apparent motion of all other stars around a stationary point in the northern sky (presently Polaris) that results from the earth's rotation. An "empty space," devoid of stars, is not found in the north. Instead, billions of stars and galaxies extend outward in all directions. Although heaven is a literal place, it has not been seen with telescopes. It may indeed exist in the northern direction, or in a distant region of the universe, or in another dimension altogether. Scripture indicates that heaven may exist entirely beyond the visible universe. In 2 Corinthians 12:2–3, the apostle Paul refers to "the third heaven"—paradise—far beyond the first heaven (Earth's atmosphere) and the second heaven (the realm of the stars). He also speaks of the Lord's having "ascended higher than all the heavens" (Eph. 4:10).

PART FIVE

General
Science

72. What is gravity?

Gravity is a force of attraction that exists between all objects. For example, the earth's gravity keeps the moon in orbit; the moon's gravity pulls back and causes the tides. The earth also pulls downward on surface objects and gives them their "weight." On the moon you would weigh six times less than on Earth, because lunar gravity is less than the earth's. Gravity acts through the vacuum of space and is the only known force strong enough to extend like invisible cords through vast distances.

On Earth, gravity causes the rain to "fall." It also makes us tired, since we work against its downward force all day. Gravity cannot be turned off; no antigravity machine has yet been invented. To experience the weightlessness of space, astronauts often train in pools of water. A few moments of artificial weightlessness can also be produced in an airplane that is flown in a loop. (Perhaps you recall the feeling from a roller-coaster ride.) It is instructive to think about what life on Earth would be like if gravity was stronger than it actually is:

Ink would drain from your pen.

No birds or planes could fly.

No tall trees or buildings could stand.

Neither evaporation nor rain would occur.

Clouds would lie on the ground as permanent fog.

Standing up would be a difficult task.

Or consider the opposite, a weakened gravity force:

We would weigh less.

A home-run baseball might fly for miles.

Earth's atmosphere would escape into space.

Oceans would evaporate.

Clearly, God has given gravity the correct strength to make life possible on Earth. Isaac Newton studied gravity three centuries ago, but modern science still does not know what really causes its force. What an incredible mystery! How do the earth and moon "know" exactly where the other is at all times and pull accordingly? Some have guessed that invisible gravity particles called gravitons stream between objects like strands of glue. We can write equations for gravity, but they are just imperfect descriptions. Whatever the mechanism, God upholds the force of gravity by his power (Col. 1:16–17; Heb. 1:3). Even those people who fail to acknowledge the God who establishes natural laws quickly learn to accept the law of gravity through experience. How much richer it is to know both the law *and* the Law-Giver!

---

73. What is light?

Simple questions in science often have complicated answers, and light is an excellent example. Light has both particle-like properties and wave properties. That is, light sometimes behaves like invisible particles called *photons.* These photons can collide with other particles such as electrons, and can be deflected like microscopic marbles. At the same time, light also displays wavelengths that act similar to water waves or sound waves, adding together or canceling. Scientists accept this unusual dual nature of light without completely understanding it.

We are all familiar with visible light. The sun produces the dramatic colors that brighten our day. Rainbows, blue skies, red sunsets—all result from the separation of sunlight into its spectral colors. However, this visible light is only a small part of the total picture. The sun and other stars also emit many kinds of light that our eyes cannot see. You have heard of some of these forms of light: radio waves and microwaves, ultraviolet and infrared, x-rays and gamma rays. All of these strange varieties of light flood our sky continually. If we could see them, the heavens would appear to be bright with energy. Although this sounds dangerous, it should be noted that the microwaves from space are just a whisper, much weaker than those produced inside a microwave oven. Also, most of the ultraviolet light and x-rays are safely absorbed by the earth's atmosphere. In recent years, instruments have been designed to detect and learn from these invisible kinds of light. For example, infrared telescopes show us many new details of stars and galaxies. Receivers for the radio waves are built in the form of huge dishes, somewhat like backyard satellite antennas. There is obviously much more light in space than "meets the eye," and each variety of light, visible and invisible, has its own story to tell about the heavens.

Light was part of the initial creation, the opposite of darkness (Gen. 1:3). God is called "light" (1 John 1:5) and "Father of the heavenly lights" (James 1:17). This is a fitting title because light is pure, beautiful, and beyond human understanding. Christians are expected to share in this image, since we are told to let our light "shine before men" (Matt. 5:16).

_____

74. What is a light-year?

This term is misleading because a light-year measures distance, not time. Many units of distance have been defined in science, and the light-year is one of the longest. It is equal to the distance that a beam of light travels in an entire year in space. The speed of light is usually given the symbol c, and can be written as $c=186,000$ miles/second (or 300,000 kilometers/second). The length of a light-year is 5.58×10^{12} miles, or roughly 6 trillion miles (about 10 trillion kilometers). This vast distance is equivalent to about 12 million round trips to the moon. A light-year also is comparable to the approximate total distance that all the motorized vehicles on Earth travel during the course of one year.

The light-year measurement is useful in describing stellar distances. The closest star to the earth (after the sun) is Alpha Centauri, 4.3 light-years away. Since this distance is 250,000 times greater than that to the sun, it is obvious that the earth is remote and isolated from the stellar heavens. A modern spacecraft would take more than 100,000 years to reach Alpha Centauri. Table 8 gives the distance to several objects in space.

_____

75. What did ancient observatories measure?

All around the world there are many ancient stone markers, which were apparently once used to measure the heavens. Since these monuments remain undisturbed today, they must have been built in the years _following_ the Genesis flood. They are found everywhere: England's

Table 8
Distance to Objects in Space

Object	Distance from Earth
Moon	1.3 light-seconds
Sun	8.3 light-minutes
Pluto	5.3 light-hours
Big Dipper stars	100 light-years (average)
Milky Way (diameter)	100,000 light-years
Andromeda	2.9 million light-years
Quasars	10 billion light-years

Stonehenge, Wyoming's Big Horn Wheel, Tonga's Coral Arch. One of their common purposes was the determination of the exact change of seasons. In particular, the stone pillars are aligned with the rising and setting of the sun at the time of the solstice. In the Northern Hemisphere, summer solstice occurs around June 21–22 each year. This is the first day of summer and also the longest day of the year. Each day during the spring the noontime sun climbs higher in the sky. Then at the solstice the sun makes a turnaround and begins heading back south. The ancients carefully measured this special day when the sun is farthest north and noon shadows are shortest. Six months later, on December 21–22, occurs the winter solstice, the Southern Hemisphere's turn for the longest day. The sun's annual path appears to move back and forth across the equator, between 23.5° North (the tropic of Cancer) and 23.5° South (the tropic of Capricorn).

The impressive, ancient stone markers show us how essential having a calendar has been to mankind throughout history. We take our wall calendars and clocks for granted, but early people did not have such luxuries. Rather, they expended great effort in building crude observatories and then they carefully watched the heavens. Measurements of objects in the heavens were needed to tell them when to plant crops and when to prepare for winter. According to the Bible, one of the reasons for the "lights" in the sky is to provide a calendar reference for days, seasons, and years (Gen. 1:14).

---

76. What's wrong with studying astrology?

Astrology is a pseudo-science based on the view that the stars and planets exert a strong influence on human affairs. It claims that the relative positions of the heavenly bodies at an individual's birth determine his or her basic makeup, and that changing astral positions can be used to predict the future. However, because the heavens were never intended for these purposes, astrology is a dangerous and wrongful practice. Stars were created for calendar keeping and for declaring God's glory. To use them otherwise is idolatry, as warned against throughout Scripture (Deut. 4:19; 2 Kings 23:5; Isa. 47:13). Astrology should not even be consulted for amusement. It is connected with the forces of evil and can lead to other occult practices and bondage to sin.

Astrology has three major flaws, each of which cancels any claim to scientific validity. First, astrology fails to succeed when tested against reality. For example, the distribution of the heavens at the moment of birth is supposed to determine one's astrological sign and thus one's personality and future. On that basis, twins should have nearly identical lives. However, twins often vary greatly in talent, personality, and the paths of life they choose. Remember Jacob and Esau (Gen. 25:19–34). Second, one's so-called astrological sign is no longer valid. Because of the precession of the earth's axis (Question 42), a person is actually born under a different star sign than is assigned by the outdated horoscopes in use today. Astrology is based on the former positions of stars (as they were 3,000 years ago in Babylonian times). Each year, the error in dating the zodiac signs grows greater. Third, it is impossible for the stars to have an effect on a person, much less on world events. The gravity of stars and planets is the only force that acts through space distances, and its effect is negligible on Earth.

---

77. Should man be in space?

Before man first walked on the moon, some skeptics warned that we would fail in the attempt. They based this on the claim that man was created to live only on the earth and that therefore God would not let us conquer space to that degree. History has shown this well-meaning prediction to be false, for—instead of failure—the lunar program (and those that followed) was successful and revealed many new details about God's universe. Space exploration continually shows how unique the earth is in comparison with other objects in space. Of course, secular science does not emphasize that point, but the testimony is nevertheless clear. For the Christian especially, every new space probe has reinforced this Bible-based appreciation of God's creation. Instead of opposing space research, it would seem that the believer has the most to gain. After all, we know that the universe is not here by chance or accident. Instead, there is design and planning in every single detail. The heavens were made for all mankind to enjoy, not for secular science to dominate.

Space exploration itself is acceptable and is in many ways similar to traveling beneath the sea. The deeper we go, the more amazing are the glories of God's creation. Although the Bible says that God has given the earth to man but the heavens are the Lord's (Ps. 115:16), this should not be taken as a "no trespassing" sign for the heavens. The earth where God has put us belongs to him as well, including everything in it (Ps. 24:1). Space travel is not forbidden in Scripture, but the earth will remain man's home even during the developing space age. The planets and moons are such hostile worlds that the visitor to these places must take along essential parts of the earth (air, food, water, fuel) to survive.

The space age has actually been beneficial to the church, especially in missions. For example, computers, a spin-off of space research, are a great aid in Bible translation. Also, satellite communications and the internet have made far-flung mission stations much less remote from their partners at home. In our day there are increasing opportunities to use technology for worthwhile purposes.

78. What are UFOs?

Unidentified flying objects—UFOs—have several possible explanations. The idea that they bring aliens from another planet is not credible, since no other life form has been discovered anywhere in the solar system. Furthermore, the earth is too isolated from all other stars besides the sun to accept the possibility of interstellar visits. There have been rumors that the United States government has secretly collected crashed flying saucers, but these stories are unfounded. Using radio-wave signals, an intense search is being conducted for life in space. Many scientists believe that life evolved on planet Earth and that it simply must have evolved elsewhere also. So far, there is no evidence to support this claim (see next question).

A more reasonable explanation of UFOs is that they result from natural events in the earth's atmosphere. For example, clouds sometimes take the unusual form of lenses. These are called *lenticular clouds,* and they have been mistaken for flying saucers. As another example, certain lightning discharges take the shape of a sphere of glowing plasma that can last for several minutes. This *ball lightning* has been seen to drift through the air and even bounce along the ground. Lenticular clouds and ball lightning are just two of dozens of natural phenomena we do not understand very well that could be sources of UFO reports. The atmosphere is very complicated, which is the reason why weather forecasting is so difficult.

Another possible origin of UFOs is the demonic world. The Bible records that Satan is able to deceive men by many schemes and can disguise himself as an angel of light (2 Cor. 2:11; 11:14). Ephesians 6:12 describes the spiritual forces of evil in heavenly realms. Two possible motives for their promotion of UFO stories come to mind. First, Satan may be trying to provide false evidence in support of evolution in space. Flying saucers lead naturally to such thinking. A second possible motive for fostering a belief in UFOs is related to end-time events. There are prophecies of unusual events in the heavens (see Question 87) and also the disappearance of believers (1 Thess. 4:13–18). Perhaps some sort of UFO activity and kidnapping plot will be popular explanations at that future time.

---

79. Is there life in space?

All efforts to detect life beyond Earth have failed so far. The search began with the moon, where 12 astronauts walked during six lunar landings from 1969 through 1972. After it was concluded that the moon was a sterile, lifeless place, the search moved to the other planets and their moons. Viking probes to Mars in 1976 performed experiments designed to detect life, including microscopic organisms, with negative results. In 1996 it was reported that a Martian meteorite found in Antarctica contained fossilized Mars bacteria. After thorough study, this claim has been rejected by most scientists. Two unmanned Voyager craft—whose destinations included Jupiter, Saturn, and Uranus—took thousands of pictures of the outer solar system. They reveal harsh, nonlivable conditions everywhere (see Question 23). Searches of deepest space have been carried out by radio telescopes, instruments that are able to beam messages of greeting toward any planets that might be circling distant stars. Radio telescopes also "listen" for space messages that may be coming in Earth's direction. During the past decades, scientists have searched dozens of nearby stars for intelligible radio signals. The results are once again completely negative. At this point, it appears that life as we know it is unique to planet Earth. This conclusion has been very upsetting to some evolutionists, who believe that life began spontaneously on Earth and that the same thing must have commonly happened elsewhere in the universe.

80. Does Scripture refer to life in space?

The Bible records that spirit beings, both good and evil, are to be found in space. Ephesians 6:12 refers to "spiritual forces of evil in the heavenly realms," and Daniel 10:12–13 gives us a glimpse of the warfare that goes on in high places. Beyond this, selected Scripture verses are sometimes also quoted in support of *physical* beings in space as distinct from the spirit world:

"Even if you have been banished to the most distant land under the heavens, from there the LORD your God will gather you" (Deut. 30:4).

"And the multitudes of heaven worship you" (Neh. 9:6).

"In that day the LORD will punish the powers in the heavens above" (Isa. 24:21).

"And he will send his angels and gather his elect from the four winds, from the ends of the earth to the ends of the heavens" (Mark 13:27).

"I have other sheep that are not of this sheep pen. I must bring them also" (John 10:16).

It is important to notice that several of these references could well refer to angels. The verses could also describe different groups of people scattered across the earth. Therefore, these texts are *not* evidence of extraterrestrial life. In contrast, Scripture in general indicates the uniqueness of the earth as a sustainer of life.

"The highest heavens belong to the LORD, but the earth he has given to man" (Ps. 115:16).

"He who fashioned and made the earth, he founded it; he did not create it to be empty, but formed it to be inhabited" (Isa. 45:18).

81. Do eggs balance on the days of equinox?

First we need some background for this unusual question. There are two days each year when the sun crosses the equator, around March 21–22 and September 21–22. At the March equinox, the sun is moving north and spring begins in that hemisphere. The Southern Hemisphere enters its fall season at the same time. This occasion is called the *vernal equinox*, named for the reawakening of plant life (in the north) and the equal periods of daylight and darkness that occur everywhere on Earth. Six months later, the hemisphere's seasons will reverse as the sun again crosses the equator, this time headed south at the time of the *autumnal equinox*.

There is a popular idea that eggs, whether fresh or hard-boiled, behave strangely on the days of the equinox. With the sun directly above the equator, gravity forces are said to be "in balance," and it is supposedly easy to stand an egg on either end. Try the experiment for yourself. To be thorough, you should also attempt to balance an egg at other times, especially around June or December when the sun is most distant from the equator. Is there any scientific basis to the egg-balancing story? No, there isn't.

Actually, the sun's gravity force could not "pull upward" on an egg as suggested. A person standing next to an egg produces a "pulling" gravity force on it 50,000 times greater than the sun, but even this human force has a negligible effect on the balancing of an egg. A steady hand can indeed make an egg balance, but it has nothing to do with the equinox date. Perhaps the story is connected with Easter eggs and their ancient symbol for spring and rebirth.

---

82. Is Procter & Gamble's symbol Satanic?

This rumor is entirely false and has been harmful to the witness of the gospel as well as unfair to Procter & Gamble. The moon-star symbol was used by the company on many of its products from 1882 to 1985. In figure 9 the stars stand for the thirteen original American colonies, and the drawing is a company logo and noth-

Figure 9
The Procter & Gamble logo

ing more. During the 1960s, a story began circulating that the corporation was controlled by Satan worshippers. The arrangement of stars in the symbol was said to secretly spell out the Revelation 13:18 "number of the beast," 666. Without examining the facts, many people signed petitions against Procter & Gamble and boycotted their products. Although the story is untrue (Procter & Gamble is owned by stockholders, not some sinister cult of moon worshippers!), the company dropped the symbol from its products in 1985, so exasperating were the false accusations and bad publicity that the logo had caused. The story continues to be circulated, mainly by misguided Christians. It is a sin to "give false testimony" (Exod. 20:16), and this rumor should not be encouraged by the faithful.

---

83. What is the strangest word in astronomy?

This distinction probably goes to the word *syzygy*, which refers to a lineup in space of three objects, such as the earth, moon, and sun (see Question 16). This particular

119

alignment occurs twice a month, during the new moon and full moon phases. Syzygy is the direct transliteration of a Greek word that appears just once in the New Testament. In Philippians 4:3, the apostle Paul uses syzygus as a term for someone at Philippi, and the word is usually translated as "true yokefellow." Paul was addressing a companion and fellow worker who was "lined up" with Paul's ministry, similar to how the word syzygy is used in modern astronomy. Various Bible commentaries propose that the original syzygus was a pastor at Philippi, a close friend, or even Paul's wife.

---

84. How is the date for Easter determined?

You have probably noticed that the date for Easter varies considerably from one year to the next. This chosen date comes from a formula established by Roman Emperor Constantine the Great and the Council of Nicaea in A.D. 325. You can use the formula to verify the date for Easter each year. First, find the vernal equinox, or first day of spring (about March 21–22), on a calendar that lists basic astronomical data. Then look for the next full moon, usually indicated in a corner box of the calendar. Easter will then fall on the following Sunday. According to this rule, the latest possible date for Easter is April 25, next occurring in 2038. The earliest is March 22, in 2285. Most often, Easter comes during the first week of April. For merchants, the changing date of Easter is inconvenient for their annual planning of sales and inventory. However, it is pleasing to realize that this special day is not determined by commerce but by the movements of the sun and moon. This agrees with the divinely ordained purpose of heavenly lights as markers for times and seasons (Gen. 1:14).

85. Are there limits to science?

There definitely are limits to what science can achieve, as confirmed both in Scripture and in the scientific method. Jeremiah 31:37 clearly implies that there are physical boundaries to what is discoverable by man: "[The Lord says:] 'Only if the heavens above can be measured and the foundations of the earth below be searched out will I reject all the descendants of Israel.'" What this passage is saying is that only *if* all of nature could be perfectly understood by man, would God's promises fail. However, because every scientific discovery leads to several new questions, God's promises are secure. In general, scientific research uncovers more new questions than it answers. True to God's word in Jeremiah, the interior of the earth remains beyond direct inspection by scientists. The earth has a radius of roughly 4,000 miles, while the deepest exploratory wells can reach only about 8 miles, or 0.2 percent of the total distance. The internal pressure and temperature of the earth are too severe for deeper study. We have not even drilled through the crust, let alone the mantle or core, which explains why such phenomena as the earth's magnetism remain poorly understood. Most of our information on the earth's interior comes from the surface study of vibrations during earthquakes. The Jeremiah passage also implies that the dimensions of the universe cannot be measured. Indeed, we see no end to space and have no way to travel to its extremes. This may be the space age, but the depths of space and their secrets remain far beyond us. The following are some other scriptural references to the limitations of science:

Scientists will never change the seasons or the cycle of day and night (Gen. 8:22).

God does great things beyond our understanding
(Job 37:5).

Man cannot alter the motions of the heavens
(Job 38:31–33).

The human mind cannot know all there is to know
(Col. 2:3).

The "scientific method" is a term describing the experimental approach to pursuing knowledge. A problem is
stated, measurements are taken, results are interpreted,
and conclusions are drawn. This is an unending process
of refinement, but final and absolute truth can never be
found scientifically. As new data is discovered, equations
and conclusions must continually be modified to fit the
changing picture. Most changes are minor refinements,
but some are major scientific breakthroughs, such as relativity and quantum theory. Since only God perfectly un-
derstands his creation, our models and equations about
nature are imperfect at best. And many areas, such as origins, miracles, and the spirit world, cannot be understood
by secular science at all. Such topics are beyond the capa-
bilities of scientists and the laboratories in which they
labor.

---

86. Can astronomy lead a person to God?

The heavens bear witness to the glory of God, and Romans 1:20 states that anyone who ignores the testimony
of creation does so "without excuse." Unfortunately,
many people are not spiritually impressed with the lessons of God's handiwork. Nor are they convinced by ful-
filled prophecy or archaeological discoveries, both of
which verify many of the details of Scripture. Although
such evidences are sufficient to make people account-

able, these facts are often not effective in changing lives. The problem is not with the evidence but with the fact that fallen human nature is blind and irrational. When people turn away from God, their understanding is "darkened" (Rom. 1:21). How else to explain why anyone would turn to secular humanism or to the occult instead of the truth?

Theologians use the term *apologetics* for the defense of the truth of Scripture. The view expressed in the previous paragraph is called presuppositional apologetics. That is, the existence of God and the inerrancy of Scripture must be accepted on faith since these truths cannot be scientifically proven in a way that will convince the skeptic. A contrasting view is called evidentialist apologetics, which holds that man *can* be intellectually convinced of spiritual truths. In other words, conversion will follow once the person has been overwhelmed with the evidence. Thomas Aquinas (1225–1274) promoted this latter view with his scientific "proofs" of the existence of God. However, his acceptance of geocentricity is a reminder that his scientific understanding was fallible. The cruel inquisition by religious leaders that Aquinas supported also shows that the intellectual, evidentialist approach to apologetics does not necessarily lead to agreement and harmony.

What, then, will bring one to a personal knowledge of the Lord? ". . . Faith comes from hearing the message, and the message is heard through the word of Christ" (Rom. 10:17). Of course, prayer also is effective in increasing one's understanding, as is the example of a consistent Christian life. Although astronomy and other scientific studies of the wonders wrought by the Creator can point one's mind in the right direction, the truth of the Word must come also through the heart.

87. Are there heavenly signs of the end times?

Scripture contains several prophecies of the changes that will occur in the sky during the final days of this present world. Table 9 presents a summary of these events. Isaiah 51:6 adds that the heavens "will vanish like smoke," and 2 Peter 3:10 states that they "will disappear with a roar." We must conclude from these biblical predictions that the present physical universe is only temporary. Signs in the heavens will be an important part of the final events on Earth.

Since the heavens have always been counted on for stability, dramatic changes in the sky will surely bring terror to many people of the future. However, the Christian, who knows the Creator of the stars, has no cause to fear such signs. In Jeremiah 10:2, the Lord says to not "be terrified by signs in the sky." A century ago, in England there occurred what has come to be called the "dark day." Unusual atmospheric conditions led to a day that remained so dark that there was widespread fear and panic about the possible arrival of the world's end. A British government assembly was in session at this time. A suggestion was made that the assembly adjourn so the men could return to their homes. One of the members then stood and made a profound statement that settled everyone down. He said that if the world was indeed at an end, it was too late to rearrange one's life. And if it was not ending, there was work to be done. The men immediately returned to the work at hand. This philosophy of life also works well for the Christian. First, be sure that your life is in order before God. Then redeem the time and work for him, instead of standing around and fearfully waiting for signs in the sky.

Table 9
Heavenly Signs of the End Times

	Isa. 13:10; 34:4 Day of the LORD	Joel 2:10, 31 Day of the LORD	Matt. 24:29, 35 Second Coming	Rev. 6:12–13 Sixth Seal	Rev. 8:10–12 Third and Fourth Trumpets
Sun	darkened	darkened	darkened	black	one-third dark
Moon	no light	dark, turned to blood	no light	blood-red	one-third dark
Stars	dissolved, no light	no light	fall	fall	one-third dark, Wormwood star falls
Heavens	rolled up like a scroll	tremble	shake, pass away	recede like a rolled up scroll	

88. Can the "music of the spheres" be explained?

This phrase is sung in the well-known hymn "This is My Father's World" by Maltbie D. Babcock (1858–1901): "All nature sings, and round me rings / The music of the spheres." The phrase was first expressed in early Greek times. It refers to music that the heavenly bodies were thought to produce as they moved across the sky. The astronomer Johannes Kepler (1571–1630) not only emphasized this heavenly music but even calculated the musical notes that the planets represented.

The idea of celestial tones has a valid basis, since musical notes are always produced by repeated regular vibrations—whether originating from vibrating strings, reeds, or drums. Human ears are sensitive to vibrations in the range of hundreds to thousands of cycles per second. As the planets circle the sun, the motion of each one is a unique form of slow, regular vibration. For example, the earth's musical frequency is an ultra-bass note of one cycle per year! The frequencies of the other planets fall on either side of this value, although all are far below our

125

threshold of hearing. Furthermore, there is no air in outer space to carry the distant sound waves to our ears. We cannot hear it, but the motion and music of the planetary spheres continues day after day. Perhaps this pure music is enjoyed by the Creator and his host of angels!

89. What quotes are pertinent for our study?

Certain statements have become well-known in that they represent the thinking of groups in the scientific community. The following collection of statements by philosophers and scientists is divided into two categories, either supporting or opposing biblical creation. The authors themselves might not agree with the category they have been placed in, but the quotations speak for themselves.

Creation View

God himself took the space of six days, for the purpose of accommodating his works to the capacity of men.

John Calvin (1554)
Commentary on Genesis

For myself, faith begins with the realization that a supreme intelligence brought the universe into being and created man. It is not difficult for me to have this faith, for it is incontrovertible that where there is a plan there is intelligence—an orderly, unfolding universe testifies to the truth of the most majestic statement ever uttered—"In the beginning God."

Arthur Compton (1936)
Chicago Daily News

I suspect that the sun is 4.5 billion years old. However, given some new and unexpected results to the contrary, and some time for frantic recalculation and theoretical readjustment, I suspect that we could live with Bishop Ussher's value for the age of the Earth and Sun. I don't think we have much in the way of observational evidence in astronomy to conflict with that.

John Eddy (1978)
Geotimes September 1978

The chance that higher life forms arose by evolutionary processes is comparable with the chance that a tornado sweeping through a junkyard might assemble a Boeing 747 from the materials therein.

Fred Hoyle (1981)
Nature November 12, 1981

The details differ, but the essential elements in the astronomical and biblical accounts of Genesis are the same: the chain of events leading to man commenced suddenly and sharply at a definite moment in time, in a flash of light and energy. . . . For the scientist who has lived by his faith in the power of reason, the story ends like a bad dream. He has scaled the mountain of ignorance; he is about to conquer the highest peak; as he pulls himself over the final rock, he is greeted by a band of theologians who have been sitting there for centuries.

Robert Jastrow (1978)
God and the Astronomers

I give thanks to thee, O Lord Creator, Who has delighted me with thy makings and . . . the works of thy hands.

Johannes Kepler (1619)
Harmonies of the World

The most beautiful system of the sun, planets, and comets, could only proceed from the counsel and dominion of an intelligent and powerful Being.

Isaac Newton (1687)
Principia

127

God did not create the planets and stars with the intention that they should dominate man, but that they, like other creatures, should obey and serve him.

Aureolus Paracelsus (1541)
Concerning the Nature of Things

We believe that God hath made all things out of nothing: because, even though the world hath been made of some material, that very same material hath been made out of nothing.

St. Augustine (A.D. 393)
Of the Faith and of the Creed

Anti-Creation View

Emotionally I am an atheist. I don't have the evidence to prove that God doesn't exist, but I so strongly suspect He doesn't that I don't want to waste my time.

Isaac Asimov (1982)
Context

Contemporary opinion on star formation holds that objects called protostars are formed as condensation from interstellar gas. This condensation process is very difficult theoretically, and no essential theoretical understanding can be claimed; in fact some theoretical evidence argues strongly against the possibility of star formation. However, we know that stars exist, and we must do our best to account for them.

J. C. Brandt (1966)
The Sun and Stars

There is a deep compulsion to believe the idea that the entire universe, including all the apparently concrete matter that assails our senses, is in reality only a frolic of convoluted nothingness, that in the end the world will turn out to be a sculpture of pure emptiness, a self-organized void.

Paul Davies (1984)
Superforce

But if the universe is really completely self-contained, having no boundary or edge, it would have neither beginning nor end: it would simply be. What place, then, for a creator?

Stephen Hawking (1988)
Brief History of Time

Even if life is not found in our solar system, there are so many other stars in space that it would *seem* that *some* of them *could* have planets around them, and it would *seem* that life *could* have arisen on *some* of the planets independently of the origin of life on the Earth [italics added].

Jay Pasachoff (1981)
Contemporary Astronomy

The Cosmos is all that is or ever was or ever will be.

Carl Sagan (1980)
Cosmos

If any planet has surface conditions suitable or at least tolerable to any terrestial organisms, life may be assumed to have developed there.

Carl Sagan and I. Shklouskii (1966)
Intelligent Life in the Universe

In the beginning was the Word, it has been piously recorded and I might venture that the word was hydrogen gas.

Harlow Shapley (1960)
Science Ponders Religion

Given so much time,
the "impossible" becomes possible,

129

The possible probable,
And the probable virtually certain,
One only has to wait:
Time itself performs the miracles.

George Wald (1954)
Scientific American

It is very hard to realize that this all is just a tiny part of an overwhelmingly hostile universe. It is even harder to realize that this present universe has evolved from an unspeakably unfamiliar early condition, and faces a future extinction of endless cold or intolerable heat. The more the universe seems comprehensible (via the big bang) the more it also seems pointless.

Steve Weinberg (1977)
The First Three Minutes

PART SIX

Technical Terms
and Ideas

90. Which is the best telescope to buy?

This is a practical question. Many beginning stargazers become discouraged because they use the wrong equipment. Just as there are different levels of reference books for the study of Scripture, so there are levels of optical tools for studying the heavens. In both cases, the best advice is to start simply and build upward from that point. One should make quality investments with lasting value. For the beginning astronomer, an initial aid might be binoculars, which should have wide-range optics and a power of about 8 to 10. (A label of 8 × 50 means that the magnification is 8, and the aperture or diameter of the front lens is 50 millimeters.) In many ways binoculars are superior to a small telescope. Binoculars are easy to use, give excellent views of the moon, planets, and star clusters, and they also work well for *indirect* viewing of solar eclipses and sunspots. *Warning:* The sun's image through binoculars should be projected onto a flat surface so it can be

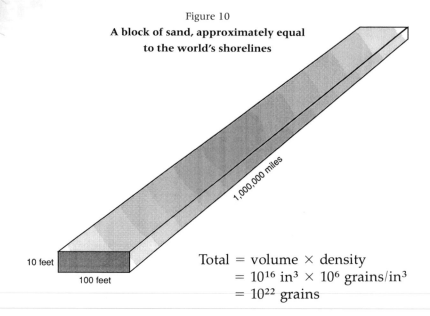

Figure 10

**A block of sand, approximately equal
to the world's shorelines**

1,000,000 miles

10 feet

100 feet

Total = volume × density
$$= 10^{16} \text{ in}^3 \times 10^6 \text{ grains/in}^3$$
$$= 10^{22} \text{ grains}$$

safely studied. After one is familiar with a binocular view of space, a small refracting or reflecting telescope can be considered. Seek some informed advice and, if possible, try out several instruments before making a purchase. The initial experiences will help the stargazer decide which telescope is best for his or her own interests.

91. Are stars as numerous as sand grains?

The promise was given to Abraham that he would be blessed with "descendants as numerous as the stars in the sky and as the sand on the seashore . . ." (Gen. 22:17). What this really means is that the seed of Abraham is beyond anyone's count, so one should not look for an exact number of descendants based on this verse. Still, the numerical comparison between stars and grains of sand provides a good illustration of the vastness of the heavens.

Table 10
Various Large-Number Estimates

Item	Size
Hairs on an average head	2×10^5
Seconds in a year	3×10^7
Retirement age in seconds	2×10^9
World population	6×10^9
Miles in a light-year	6×10^{12}
Words spoken since creation	10^{16}
Sand grains on all the seashores	10^{22}
Observed stars	10^{22}
Water drops in all the oceans	10^{25}
Candle power of the sun	3×10^{27}
Electrons in the observed universe	10^{80}

Let us consider a rough estimate for all the sand grains on the seashores of planet Earth. We will depict this total as a block of sand that is 10 feet deep, 100 feet wide, and 1,000,000 miles long. This length equals 42 trips around the world, a generous figure for the extent of the world's sandy beaches. The total volume of this block is found by multiplying the three dimensions, which is represented as 5.28×10^{12} ft^3 = 10^{16} in^3. A one-inch cube of average sand contains about 1,000,000 grains (assuming that there are 100 grains lined along each edge). The total number of grains in the imaginary block of sand is depicted in figure 10.

This is the number 1 followed by 22 zeros, which may be expressed as 10 billion trillion sand grains. Surprisingly, the very same number is used by astronomers to approximate the total number of known stars, including all galaxies. The stars are indeed as numerous as the sands on the seashores. God's family is large—and growing!

To help us understand vast numbers such as 10^{22}, table 10 lists some other large-number estimates.

92. Are relativity and quantum theories correct?

These two fields of study revolutionized physics during the last century. The older science of Isaac Newton's time is called classical physics. The twentieth century marked the dramatic change from classical to modern physics. Relativity theory refers to the modification of basic equations that is needed when high speeds are involved. As particles move close to the speed of light, their mass, size, speed, and time all behave in the strange new ways predicted by Albert Einstein's relativity theory. In physics, the term *relativity* basically means that the particles' properties can change relative to the motion. However, for the typical speeds of life, even during the space age, classical physics still produces excellent agreement with reality.

Quantum theory explains how particles interact and exchange energy. It was first formulated by the German physicist Max Planck (1858–1947) a century ago. Quantum theory is very fundamental to science—because we are all made of small particles! A quantum is a tiny amount of energy that cannot be further subdivided. Experiments have shown that energy is always exchanged in these small bundles, or quanta. One troubling part of quantum theory is that some questions in science become unknowable because the exact behavior of atomic particles is unpredictable and unmeasurable. This apparent randomness to nature bothered Einstein greatly. In his thinking, quantum theory seemed to rule out God's control and foreknowledge of all things. In Einstein's words, he could not believe that "God plays dice with the universe." Einstein believed that all of science should have predictable cause-and-effect results, as it does in classical physics.

Relativity and quantum theories have become foundation stones in modern physics. Hundreds of different experiments seem to verify their correctness. One can analyze these same experiments within a classical framework, but the results are often forced and complicated. Some scientists continue to reject these new fields of science for philosophical/religious reasons and prefer to interpret modern physics in terms of the older, classical approach. Such efforts are welcome, because they provide checks and balances against possible errors in scientific thinking. However, relativity and quantum theories are elegant and powerful ideas. It is certainly rash to limit God by saying that he cannot operate his universe by using these principles or others yet undiscovered. The philosophical problems that seem to arise from relativity and quantum physics may actually be due to mankind's limitations. What appears random or mysterious to us is a certainty to God, who made the particles and the rules of nature in the first place.

---

93. What is the anthropic principle?

This popular term in astronomy comes from the Greek word for man, *anthropos*. For any principle of science to be acceptable, there must be experimental results with general validity. The anthropic principle states that the universe is especially suited for the well-being of mankind; it is "user-friendly." As just one of hundreds of examples, consider the tides that the moon causes on the earth. If the moon was closer to the earth, tides would be greatly increased. Ocean waves could then sweep across the continents. The seas themselves might heat to the boiling point from the resulting friction. On the other hand, a more distant moon would reduce the tides. Marine life then would be endangered by the resulting preponderance of stagnant water. Mankind would also be in trouble because the oxygen in the air we breathe is replenished by marine plants.

We can conclude that the moon *is* in just the "correct" position for our well-being. Even such details as the mass of protons and the strength of gravity have values that give stability to the universe and thus reinforce the anthropic principle.

The anthropic principle is a powerful argument that the universe was *designed*. Of course, whether looking at an intricate watch or a beautiful planet, any design requires a designer. Evolutionary theory believes it has an answer to "design" in biological systems by hypothesizing ongoing processes of mutation and natural selection. Living things are said to change very slowly and to improve with time. There are many fundamental problems with the evolution worldview, not the least of which is that—in the case of the anthropic principle—the view provides no answer at all. Whether describing tides, proton mass, or the earth's position in the solar system, a grand design is present from the very beginning. These phenomena do not mutate or change with time. The negative response of secular science to new evidences of design is interesting in that it shows the extremes to which some will go to maintain a belief in the random origin of all things. For example, it has been proposed that there really is an infinite number of universes, each one with a completely different set of physical properties. According to such thinking, our particular universe just happens to have conditions suitable for human life, and that is why we are here to enjoy it! Of course, there is no way to detect any "other" universes or comprehend their underlying principles. Scripture describes the creation of just one universe. It contains everything, including the clear marks of the supremely intelligent design of our Creator God.

Consider two further examples of the anthropic principle that display the careful design of the universe. *The first involves the mass of a proton.* Although this subatomic particle might at first seem to be of trivial significance, closer

136

inspection reveals that the proton's mass is exactly what is needed to provide both its own stability and that of the entire universe. In contrast, a free neutron (n) (which is a slightly heavier particle) decays into a proton (p), an electron (e), and an antineutrino $(\bar{v})$ with a half-life of just 12 minutes. This decay can be written as

$$n \rightarrow p + e + \bar{v}$$

Free neutrons simply cannot persist in nature. However, if the mass of a proton could be somehow increased by just 0.2 percent, the proton would become the unstable parti-cle and would quickly decay into a neutron, positron (e^{+}), and neutrino (v). This would be represented as

$$p \rightarrow n + e^{+} + v$$

This second reaction does *not* occur, but it *would* if the pro-ton were just *slightly* heavier.

The implications of proton mass are truly universal. Of chief significance is that the hydrogen nucleus is composed of just a single proton. Thus, the hypothesized rapid decay of protons would destroy all hydrogen atoms. Further-more, hydrogen is a major component of our bodies, water molecules, the sun, and all other stars. In fact, hydrogen is the dominant element of the universe. It is obvious that the proton's mass seems to have been wisely planned to be slightly smaller than that of a neutron, in order to pre-vent the total collapse of the universe! Note also that pro-tons are not subject to the influence of mutation or natu-ral selection. Their physical properties were chosen from the very beginning of time and have not changed.

The second design example involves the gravity force. All masses are found to attract each other, with a force that varies inversely as the square of the separation distance between the masses:

$$\text{Gravity Force} \sim \frac{1}{(\text{Separation Distance})^2}$$

Scientists have long wondered about the factor of 2 in this expression. It simply looks "too neat." In an evolved universe, one would not expect such a simple relationship. For example, why isn't the distance factor 1.99 or 2.001? The gravity force has been repeatedly tested with sensitive torsion balances, showing that the factor is indeed precisely 2, at least to five decimal places, 2.00000. Any value other than 2 would lead to an eventual catastrophic decay of orbits and of the entire universe. As does the proton mass, the gravity force clearly displays elegant and essential design. Proton mass and gravity strength are just two of the invisible wonders that surround us in the universe. Praise is due the Creator for the delicate details that make possible our very existence in the world he created.

---

94. Did Supernova 1987A actually occur?

In 1987 a new supernova, or exploding star, was observed in the night sky. It was located in the Large Magellanic Cloud, a galaxy about 180,000 light-years away. How can one explain this event on a short time scale? Did the supernova actually take place?

The options of decaying light speed and relativistic cosmology (see Question 61) would allow for observing the distant event on a short time scale. The mature creation view suggests that the complete supernova display may have been built directly into the created light waves. Then, did the 1987 supernova actually take place? The answer involves our understanding of time. God's omniscience places him completely above time. He simultaneously sees the past, present, and future. The creation of the supernova signal in transit could thus be taken to mean that it *did* take place in the mind of God.

There is an alternative view. Evidence shows that, at some point in history, radioactive decay was temporarily accelerated. This may have occurred at the time of the curse or the flood. If atoms were "reprogrammed" in this way, the fundamental change may also have extended to the heavens above. That is, an appearance of age may have been built into the universe at this time. In this case, the universe suddenly was filled with aging stars and supernova remnants, much as we observe today.

---

95. What are cosmic strings?

Some astrophysicists believe that there are "superstrings" of mass-energy throughout space. These are long strands of unknown matter, existing in one to nine different space dimensions. This complex mathematical description means that they cannot be observed directly. We only know of four dimensions in nature, including three-dimensional space and time. These cosmic strings are said to form closed loops in space, millions of light-years in size. Energetic elementary particles are visualized as knots or vibrations in these strings.

Cosmic strings have been proposed to explain the origin and distribution of galaxies following the assumed big bang. Somehow the presence of these strings long ago gathered primordial matter into clumps. It is further hoped that superstring theory will eventually bring about a unification of all the properties of elementary particles and the forces between them. Some experts boldly predict that a fundamental "theory of everything" will eventually be developed. However, it is an open question whether the existence of cosmic strings will be verified. Instead, the string concept may be replaced by new ideas even more abstract. Already, some physicists are describing invisible *membranes* in space instead of superstrings. Such efforts to understand the universe should be an encouragement for the creationist, who already knows that "The heavens declare the glory of God; the skies proclaim the work of his hands" (Ps. 19:1).

---

96. Is there a basic building block for matter?

Particle accelerators have been used to study high-energy physics since the 1930s. Protons, for example, are given high speeds and are then directed against targets of various materials. The resulting interactions provide a probe of the microscopic world. Large accelerators are now able to achieve penetration of an atomic nucleus and even to subdivide individual protons and neutrons. What results from these interactions is a shower of more than 150 different "elementary" particles, which exhibit a bewildering array of speeds, masses, electrical charges, and lifetimes. Their names include muons, neutrinos, pions, and quarks. Given the hierarchy of ever deeper levels seen within the atom, one might predict that modern science will never reach the bottom-level building blocks of nature. Instead, the inner layers of complexity seem to continue without any limit. It is like trying to peel an onion; there is always another layer underneath! (See figure 11). Of course, similar layers of complexity are also observed in the heavens above. Such results are to be expected in the work of an infinite Creator.

One consequence of accelerating protons to high-energy levels is to effectively increase their temperature. In this way, physicists are attempting to mimic, on a small scale, the energetic conditions they think existed at the earliest moments of the proposed big bang chronology. Of course, this interpretation is not essential to particle experiments,

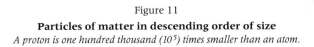

Figure 11
Particles of matter in descending order of size
A proton is one hundred thousand (10^5) times smaller than an atom.

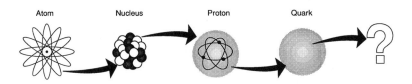

| Atom | Nucleus | Proton | Quark |

even though it gets the most publicity. Alternately, discoveries of the inner atom can be taken to reveal something of the complexity that came into being at the instant of the supernatural creation. Therefore, the creationist need not oppose high-energy experiments, but—on the contrary—can truly enjoy the exciting search for order in nature. As with the stars above, the microscopic details of God's handiwork are most appreciated by those who know him.

---

97. Is the speed of light decreasing?

This idea has been suggested by several creation scientists. They believe that the speed of light was infinite at the time of creation but then began decreasing at the time of Adam and Eve's sin, when the curse was imposed on nature. Since then, this speed *(c)* has decayed and slowed to its present value, of c = 300,000 kilometers/second (186,000 miles/second). If true, a changing speed of light could solve a number of technical problems that creationists deal with. For example, faster light could have traveled from the distant galaxies to the earth very rapidly. Since light speed is connected with other constants of nature, the implications of a changing light speed are very significant. Many other findings of science would be

141

affected by a variable light speed, including the law of conservation of energy.

Historical measurements of light speed made over the last 300 years have been examined. Other constants of nature that should have changed in parallel with c have also been looked at. Thus far the results are not conclusive. Before creationists give major support to a decaying speed of light, more study is advisable. In particular, the following points should be kept in mind:

1. Many scientists worldwide have looked for evidence of a changing light speed during this century, without success.
2. Early measurements of c are very important in the search for changing light speed. However, early measurements of c have large uncertainties.
3. Equations that tentatively have been fit to light decay data are very complicated. They include logarithms, sine functions, and other constants. However, decay formulas in nature usually display a simple exponential curve.
4. We do not see any change occurring in the speed of light today. This raises the question of why light speed would have just recently settled down to a constant value.

The decay of the speed of light is a revolutionary idea in science. Because of its many implications, both scientific and theological, caution is needed in accepting or promoting it. Creationists look forward to the results of further study of this topic.

A further comment is needed concerning the speed of light and the creation of the heavens. God made the sun, moon, and stars on the fourth day (Gen. 1:14–19). Their created light was fully spread out across space (see Question 61). Thus one could say that light speed was infinite at the moment of creation. This light then probably was given the speed c that we measure today.

---

98. Does the HR diagram prove that the universe is old?

The HR (Hertzsprung-Russell) diagram (figure 12) shows the distribution of stars with various surface temperatures and brightnesses. The stars are found to group into three specific categories:

Main-sequence stars (1)	"average" stars, such as the sun
Red giants (2)	large, bright "cool" stars
White dwarfs (3)	small, dim "hot" stars

Stellar evolution theory assumes that stars slowly change between these three categories as they age and that each stage of star development lasts for millions or

Figure 12

Hertzsprung-Russell Diagram of Star Distribution

Each data point on the diagram represents a star with a particular temperature (horizontal axis) and brightness (vertical axis).

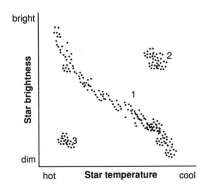

143

billions of years. Since all three types of stars are seen in abundance in the night sky, secular science concludes that the universe must be ancient.

The creationist has two rebuttals to this idea. First, based on the biblical record, the stars were likely created in all their variety from the very beginning of time: ". . . star differs from star in splendor" (1 Cor. 15:41)—that includes temperature (color) and brightness. Second, stars may be aging faster than current models suggest. We don't really know the rate of stellar aging, either in the past or in the present.

An HR diagram can also be drawn for the stars within a particular star cluster. When this is done, one often finds examples of stars that are in an apparent transition stage. That is, their temperature and brightness places them on the diagram between the main-sequence and red giant stars. This pattern is used to promote a multibillion-year age for the clusters. A creationist's reply is once again that the stars are actually all the same age and were formed a few thousand years ago when the universe was just four days old. Since then, the more massive stars may have aged more rapidly and therefore left the main-sequence category.

---

99. What is gravitational collapse?

"Gravitational collapse" is proposed by some scientists as an alternate, non-nuclear energy source for the sun and stars (see Question 31). The theory was worked out a century ago by physicists Helmholtz and Kelvin, *before* nuclear energy was discovered. Today, although nuclear fusion is almost universally believed to fuel the stars, detailed studies of the sun have raised questions about this assumption. The fusion of hydrogen into helium produces an intense flood of subatomic particles called neutrinos. On that basis, one would expect neutrinos from the sun to reach the earth in vast numbers. However, after years of careful measuring, scientists have simply not detected the expected amounts of solar neutrinos. As a result, a few scientists doubt that fusion is the dominant energy source for the stars.

The next most likely source of star energy is gravitational contraction. A very slow shrinking of the sun's size would release vast amounts of heat, as potential energy is converted into kinetic motion of atoms. A radius shrinkage of just .009 feet/hour or 80 feet/year would produce the total amount of observed solar energy. (Question 32 deals with efforts to measure such a change in the sun's size.) Since this alternate energy source could only supply the sun's energy for a few million years, it has been totally rejected by secular astronomy. This is a case where long-age thinking severely limits the options of science. Perhaps the real source of solar energy is some combination of both gravitational collapse and nuclear fusion.

Gravitational contraction can also be applied to the planet Jupiter, a large planet that is observed to give off more heat than it receives from the sun. A surface contraction of just one centimeter per year would account for the measured heat flow from Jupiter. However, because this change is too small to measure, we do not know whether or not Jupiter is actually experiencing gravitational collapse.

---

100. Are dying stars a part of the curse in Genesis?

According to the Genesis account, when Adam and Eve sinned, man's relationship with God was dramatically changed. Death entered the world through sin (Rom.

5:12), with both spiritual and physical dimensions. The world became a more difficult place in which to live. Genesis 3 describes some of the physical changes that took place, including the growth of "thorns and thistles." From a perfect beginning, life became a struggle; deterioration set in and has been present ever since. Scientists have quantified a law of nature that can be seen as a reflection of God's curse. It is called the second law of thermodynamics, and there are many ways to express it:

Order in the universe is decreasing.

Entropy, a measure of disorder, is increasing.

Energy is becoming unavailable.

Energy transfer processes are wasteful.

Everything wears out.

Scripture also describes this aging and decaying of all things. Notice that some of the references include the realm of the heavens:

"All men are like grass,
    and all their glory is like the flowers of the field;
the grass withers and the flowers fall,
    but the word of the Lord stands forever."

1 Peter 1:24–25

For the creation was subjected to frustration, not by its own choice, but by the will of the one who subjected it, in hope that the creation itself will be liberated from its bondage to decay and brought into the glorious freedom of the children of God. We know that the whole creation has been groaning as in the pains of childbirth right up to the present time.

Romans 8:20–22

[The heavens] will perish, but you remain;
   they will all wear out like a garment.
Like clothing you will change them
   and they will be discarded.

Psalm 102:26

"Heaven and earth will pass away, but my words will never pass away."

Mark 13:31

Lift up your eyes to the heavens,
   look at the earth beneath;
the heavens will vanish like smoke,
   the earth will wear out like a garment
   and its inhabitants die like flies.
But my salvation will last forever,
   my righteousness will never fail.

Isaiah 51:6

It seems clear—from both observation and Scripture—that stars take part in the overall degeneration of the universe. But is star aging actually a part of the "curse"? Were stars originally intended to shine forever? Several comments can be made regarding the available options:

1. *If stars originally had the potential to last forever, then some process of perfect energy recycling was needed.* An absence of the entropic disordering process is difficult to comprehend, but our minds are limited! In a parallel way, partaking of the Tree of Life would have given Adam and Eve permanent life, yet we cannot understand how a person's nonglorified physical body could last forever without wearing out.

2. *Although the stars of today are temporary, Scripture seems to indicate permanent stars in the eternal state:*

147

Those who are wise will shine like the brightness of the heavens, and those who lead many to righteousness, like the stars for ever and ever.

Daniel 12:3

He set them [stars] in place for ever and ever;
he gave a decree that will never pass away.

Psalm 148:6

The new, eternal heavens and earth are mentioned in Revelation 21:1. They will surely be very different from the universe that we know.

3. *Some aspects of the law of entropy must have been in operation before God's curse* (for example the eating of fruit and plants). Similarly, stars (like plants) did not necessarily completely take part in the death sentence mentioned in Romans 5:12. The common terms "dying stars" and "the death of stars" are perhaps misleading. Stars wear out, but they do not die in the same way animals do. Stars may have aged from the very beginning of the creation. We must remember that the second law of thermodynamics is man's imperfect model of nature's behavior. The actual curse may entail more of nature than the second law includes—or maybe less.

4. *Stars were created in great variety: "normal" stars, white dwarfs, and red giants.* This may be part of the internal integrity and consistency of God's universe. A parallel may be found within the Garden of Eden. Trees were surely created with fruit in various stages of development. If all the fruit had been either ripe or unripe, there would have been a food-supply problem for our first parents.

More study is needed concerning the relationship between God's curse and the law of entropy. In both theology and science, many related questions remain unanswered. Meanwhile, an attitude of caution is needed in drawing conclusions in this area. God's ways, including the full implications of the curse, are beyond our understanding. Figure 13 outlines this discussion.

Figure 13
God's curse and the law of entropy

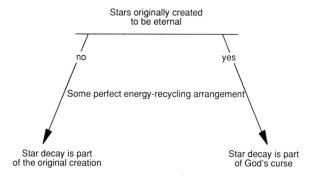

PART SEVEN

Additional Astronomy
Questions

101. Who were some pioneer creationist astronomers?

Biblical astronomers have made many important discoveries. Their testimonies are an encouragement to Christians and also a reminder to everyone of the creation heritage of astronomy. The following men and women are selected from among many others. They may be unfamiliar today, but they were household names during their lifetimes.

Arthur Eddington (1882–1944) was trained in astronomy at the British Royal Observatory in Greenwich, England. He pioneered work in astrophysics with an emphasis on stellar structure. Eddington was the first to calculate the large diameter of red giant stars, including Betelgeuse, later verified with telescopes. In 1919 he measured the bending of starlight during a solar eclipse, thus verifying Einstein's general relativity theory. Eddington grew up in a quiet Quaker home and maintained a strong pietistic faith all his life. In his publications Eddington taught that creation needed to be measured, explored, and appreciated. In *Science and the Unseen World* (1929) he declared that the meaning of life was to be found in spiritual reality rather than in scientific data alone. He believed that the spiritual realm was just as real as the world of nature. He scoffed at philosophical proofs, whether for or against God's existence. He wrote, "The most flawless proof of the existence of God is no substitute for [our relationship with him] . . . if we have that relationship, the most convincing disproof is turned harmlessly aside."

David Fabricius (1564–1617) was a Dutch astronomer who discovered the first known variable star in 1596, which was later named Mira. It is located in the December constellation Cetus. Fabricius watched the light output of Mira slowly change during 1596. Today Mira is thought to expand and contract over a 331-day period somewhat like a soap bubble, with varying brightness. Fabricius had a friendship with both Tycho Brahe and Johannes Kepler. He also was the minister of a local Dutch Reformed church. Faith in God and preaching duties held first place in Fabricius's life. Astronomy was a secondary interest in which the Lord blessed Fabricius with Mira's discovery.

Pierre Gassendi (1592–1655) was a personal friend of the astronomer Galileo. Gassendi was the first to observe a planetary transit across the face of the sun, that of Mercury in 1631. This particular observation helped verify Kepler's laws of planetary motion. Gassendi also experimented with the principle of inertia and helped explain this universal tendency of objects to remain at rest or in constant motion. He introduced the term *aurora borealis* in 1621 to describe the northern and southern lights. He further supported Galileo's heliocentric idea that God directed the earth to revolve about the sun. Gassendi believed God had created the atoms of the universe in a single stroke. He correctly taught that the creation was open to detailed scientific analysis. Gassendi also insisted that man had an immaterial soul, which made man distinct from the animal world.

Caroline Herschel (1750–1848) lived in the shadow of her brother William and also her astronomer nephew John Herschel. William discovered the planet Uranus in 1781 while Caroline worked as his astronomy assistant. She diligently taught herself the mathematical details of the heavens and soon began her own observations. Caroline catalogued 14 new nebulae, including what is today called the Andromeda Galaxy. Between 1786 and 1797 she discovered eight new comets, an outstanding accomplishment. The British Royal Astronomical Society voted Caroline a gold medal in 1828 and later made her an honorary member. All her life Caroline Herschel displayed a solid Christian testimony. She composed her own epitaph, including these words on her grave in Hanover, Germany:

> Here lies the earthly veil of Caroline Herschel.
>   The eyes of her who passed to glory,
> while below turned to the starry heavens.
>   [She followed] to a better life her father, Isaac Herschel.

Henrietta Swan Leavitt (1868–1921) developed a childhood interest in astronomy. This eventually led to her life's work at the Harvard College Observatory in Cambridge, Massachusetts. She discovered four new novae or exploding stars, and catalogued more than 2,400 variable stars. Miss Leavitt had a special interest in the properties of Cepheid variable stars. These important stars reveal their distance by the way their light output changes with time. She calibrated this distance method, thus providing an important yardstick for measuring the depths of space. Cepheid variables remain today one of the most popular techniques for finding distances to stars and galaxies. Throughout her life Henrietta Leavitt remained loyal to her pastor father and also to her Puritan roots. Biographer Solon Bailey describes her as "a devoted member of her immediate family circle . . . unselfishly considerate in her friendships, steadfastly loyal to her principles and deeply conscientious and sincere in her Christian life and character."

Maria Mitchell (1818–1889) was the first woman astronomer in America. Her discovery of Comet Mitchell in 1847 called attention to the role of American women in science. She was educated chiefly by her father, then enjoyed a distinguished career as an astronomy professor at Vassar College in New York. All her life Maria presented a strong testimony to the creation. She wrote, "Every formula which expresses a law of nature is a hymn of praise to God." Her diary further states that "There is a God and He is good . . . I try to increase my trust in this, my only article of creed." At her birthplace in Massachusetts, the Maria Mitchell Association today maintains an observatory, library, and science museum.

Thomas Wright (1711–1786) studied astronomy in eighteenth-century England. Immanuel Kant credits Wright for originating the disk-shaped model for the Milky Way Galaxy, the picture still valid today. Wright also correctly understood that the universe was made up of numerous galaxies. He worked diligently to integrate scientific observation with biblical theology. While the telescope could show universe structure, Wright believed that religion alone could provide the correct cosmological overview. In one of Wright's early models God's abode was placed at the physical center of the universe, with the far-distant outer darkness of space as a place of punishment.

_____

102. Does the seven-day week support creation?

The earth's motion provides two natural divisions of time. One rotation or complete turn of the earth defines the 24-hour day. One orbital revolution around the sun defines our year. The week is a third, intermediate time segment that is not readily derived from observations. There is no obvious seven-day rhythm in the solar system or space beyond. Attempts to find an origin for the week in moon phases or in seven distinct astronomical objects are unconvincing. Our week appears to be a direct reflection of the calendar cycle ordained by God in Genesis 2:2–3.

Alternate calendar groupings of days have been attempted in the past. In 1792 France instituted a new decimal calendar with a ten-day week. Each day was further divided into decimal parts instead of hours and minutes. This calendar failed to satisfy French citizens and disappeared after just 14 years of use. In 1929 Russia also attempted to dissociate the week from its religious basis by simply eliminating Saturdays and Sundays from the calendar. Soviet people enjoy weekends just like everyone else and this unpopular calendar was also short-lived, lasting only one year. Surely the enduring seven-day week is a strong testimony to the reliability of the creation account.

---

103. How did the Star of David originate?

This popular Jewish symbol is a six-pointed star formed by two overlapping equilateral triangles. It appears on many synagogues and also on the national flag of Israel. The star symbol is very old and was used as a decoration by many ancient cultures, from Britain to Mesopotamia. The oldest known example dates from about 6000 B.C. During the Middle Ages the symbol became connected with magic and protection, along with the pentagram or five-pointed star. The Star of David also came to be called the *Shield of David* or the *Seal of Solomon*, although its use by these leaders is doubtful. The Star of David is not men-

155

tioned in Scripture. During the last two centuries the six-pointed star has become a distinct Jewish symbol. One motive was the desire to have a common Jewish identification similar to the Christian cross. Although the Nazis used the star as a badge of shame during World War II, it came to represent unity and hope. Today the Star of David stands alongside the much older *menorah* or candelabrum as a symbol of Jewish tradition.

104. What is Arizona's meteorite crater like?

The Barringer Crater is located in the desert plains of north central Arizona. This large depression is nearly a mile across and 600 feet deep. For many years there was a lively debate over the crater's origin, whether volcanic in nature or the result of an impact collision.

Iron fragments found in the area verify the impact of a large meteorite, perhaps 50 feet in diameter and weighing about 12,000 tons. Most of the space rock was vaporized and quickly disappeared. Energy released in the collision was equal to 10 to 20 megatons of dynamite, roughly equivalent to the entire 1980 Mount St. Helens volcanic eruption.

Besides the origin of the crater, a second historical debate concerns the crater's age. There is a wide range of published age estimates, anywhere between 800 and 200,000 years. The most popular value today is a 50,000-year history for the crater. However, not everyone agrees. In particular, Hopi Indians living in the area have a legend that the crater formed just a few centuries ago. They also describe observations by their ancestors of a fiery descent from heaven, that is, a meteorite fall, long before modern scientists recognized the impact origin.

The widespread uncertainty about the crater's age clearly shows the inability of science to absolutely date the past. The lesson is one of caution in accepting long-age chronologies for any past events on the earth.

---

105. What are moon rocks like?

During 1969 to 1972, the Apollo astronauts brought nearly 2,000 rock samples, weighing 842 pounds total, back from the moon. Since the Apollo program cost $24 billion, one might value the moon rocks at $28.5 million per pound! Some of these rocks can be seen today in major museums. The three types of collected samples are crystalline rock, soil, and breccia (pronounced bresha). Most of the lunar rock is basalt, which is also common on Earth. This dark, fine-grained igneous rock forms when molten lava cools quickly. The visible dark areas of the moon, called *lunar seas,* are vast areas where lava has flowed and hardened into basalt. There are still occasional sightings of lunar volcanic activity. The lighter *lunar highlands* fringing many craters are mountains of material tossed upward by meteorite impacts. The lunar soil consists of powdered remains of past collisions between meteorites and the moon surface. Many small beads of quartz indicate melting of rock material during these impacts. These beads help the moon as a reflector of sunlight. The breccia is made of larger rock fragments. The lunar samples contain similar materials to Earth, although the moon has a higher amount of heat-resistant elements such as calcium, aluminum, and titanium.

There is no sedimentary rock on the moon since liquid water is completely lacking. Small amounts of water in the form of ice may exist within some moon craters, probably the result of comet collisions. During the years of lunar history since creation, the moon has experienced many meteorite collisions, both large and small. There is

157

also an absence of granite and the elements carbon and oxygen, all very common materials on Earth.

The moon makes a good night light but not a good garden. There were early reports that moon soil had almost magical growing properties for plants. Some even concluded that the moon was not cursed like the earth and therefore should have ideal growing conditions. These ideals have no biblical basis because the curse extends throughout the universe according to Romans 8:19–21. Lunar soil will indeed support healthy plant growth, but only if water, carbon dioxide, and other nutrients are added.

The moon, supernaturally made on the fourth day of creation, certainly has no appearance of being in a pure, unfallen state. One cannot help but consider the extreme contrasts between the comfortable earth and its inhospitable satellite companion.

---

106. Is the moon receding from the earth?

The moon's average distance from the earth is indeed increasing slightly, about 1.5 inches each year. This effect is due to gravity interaction between the earth and moon. Lunar tides slightly slow the earth's rotation by about .005 seconds each year. The moon in turn feels a slight forward push that gradually increases its orbit size.

In the recent-creation view the moon's distance has not changed significantly since its formation. During a span of 10,000 years, for example, lunar recession amounts to only about a quarter mile. On an evolutionary time scale, however, serious problems arise. Far back in evolutionary history, tides and the resulting lunar recession would have been much greater. Extrapolating backward in time one finds the moon to be very close to the earth, if not actually touching it, in less than two billion years. There is no evidence to indicate that such a close lunar approach has ever occurred. One result would be a severe heating and boiling away of the oceans due to friction from gravity. The moon appears to have remained close to its present position over its entire lifetime. Data such as this seriously calls into question the assumed long ages of evolutionary history.

107. Is there a face on Mars?

The quick answer is *no*. Claims of sculptured shapes on the surface of Mars are simply false. One particular Martian mountain has somewhat the appearance of a face when sunlight hits it at a low angle. This feature was first photographed by the U.S. Viking space probe in 1976. However, what appear to be facial features are actually natural ridges and craters. With more direct sunlight, any resemblance to an image on the mountain completely disappears. Additional reports of pyramids and other artificial shapes on Mars are likewise false. There seems to be an extreme effort by some people to promote the possibility of alien civilizations. However, such evidence is completely lacking, whether on Mars or anywhere else beyond the earth.

108. Why is the sky dark at night?

As simple as this question sounds, it is not trivial. The answer involves much more than the absence of the sun at night. Our evening sky is filled with stars. If this star-filled space extends sufficiently far, then no matter in which direction one looks, the line of sight should intercept a star. Distant stars and galaxies are faint, of course,

159

but there are many more of them. Between every two stars there is another star. As an analogy, consider a forest. If you are completely surrounded, then you will see continuous trees and branches in all directions.

It would seem that the entire night sky should be a brilliant glare of starlight. If true, however, the resulting heat and radiation would quickly extinguish all life on Earth. The obvious darkness of night is called *Olbers' Paradox*. Physician and astronomer Wilhelm Olbers first described this problem in 1823. There are several proposed solutions. *First,* there may be a finite number of stars and galaxies. Then, like a limited number of trees in a forest, one might see the darkness beyond. A *second* solution involves the redshift of starlight (see Question 66). If the galaxies are all expanding outward, then their light may be shifted completely beyond the visible range. Indeed, the sky is filled with radio waves that have a wavelength greater than visible light. *Third,* there may be obscuring gas or dust clouds that hide distant stars. This explanation is usually rejected because, on an evolutionary time scale, the interstellar material would gradually heat up and would itself glow brightly.

Today the most popular dark-sky explanation involves the big bang theory. It is thought that an early, rapid, inflationary expansion of the universe pushed many stars so far outward that their light has not yet reached the earth. Whatever the correct answer to Olbers' Paradox, there are creationist alternatives to the big bang interpretation. In the end, it must be concluded that God gave us dark night skies for our enjoyment and survival.

---

109. What is dark matter?

This term refers to an unknown form of matter, perhaps small particles or radiation. It is thought to exist throughout space, but thus far remains undetected. This mysterious matter is needed to solve at least two distinct astronomy problems.

First, galaxies do not appear to have nearly enough mass to hold themselves together. It is the gravity attraction of matter that provides stability for space objects. To maintain galaxy shape over evolutionary time, these star groups must have much more mass than is visible. In fact, as much as 90 percent of their needed mass is unaccounted for.

Second, all of interstellar space is thought to be permeated with hidden matter. This additional material is needed to give the universe a closed nature. That is, most cosmological models assume that the universe will eventually cease expanding, then gradually fall back together. As with individual galaxies, a great deal more mass is needed than presently is known to exist for closure of the universe.

Astronomers are certain that vast quantities of *dark, hidden,* or *cold* matter exist. In fact they have largely abandoned the more tentative label, *missing* mass. Although required in evolutionary astronomy, the proposed additional space material is optional to the creation view. In the creation view galaxies have not existed long enough to disintegrate, and the universe is not necessarily closed in nature.

Many hidden forms of matter may indeed exist. However, their eventual detection would not solve the many problems of an evolutionary formation of stars, galaxies, or the universe itself.

---

110. What is Biosphere II?

This facility was built as a self-sustaining enclosure located near Tucson, Arizona. Biosphere I is said to be the earth itself. At a cost of $200 million, the large "terrarium" Biosphere II contains a million-gallon ocean, a small rainforest, and farmland. Also introduced were 3,000 species of plants and animals.

In 1991 a two-year experiment began with eight volunteers who entered Biosphere II. The purpose was to "maintain resilient, persistent, complex, evolving ecosystems." It was to be a modern Garden of Eden, in preparation for eventual space colonization. However, the results were discouraging. Fresh oxygen was needed from outside the enclosure to replace losses. Much of the wildlife died, including the birds. Meanwhile, ants and cockroaches thrived and multiplied throughout the enclosure. The ocean became acidic and freshwater supplies became salty. The volunteers finally abandoned the project, having lost an average of 25 pounds each.

A second biosphere experiment began in 1994 and lasted just two months. This time the human occupants had severe personality conflicts and fights occurred between them. One volunteer commented upon leaving the facility, "It is hard to play God."

The obvious conclusion is that the creation is very complex and interdependent, including human relationships. These experiments raise serious questions about the ability of astronauts to ever colonize space. Biosphere II is now managed by Columbia University as a research laboratory and tourist attraction.

Suggested Resources
for Astronomy and Creation

Publications

Acts and Facts magazine (Institute for Creation Research, P.O. Box 2667, El Cajon, CA 92021). Contains articles on many Bible-science topics.

Astronomy and Creation, 1995 (Don DeYoung, Creation Research Society Books, P.O. Box 8263, St. Joseph, MO 64508). A somewhat more technical summary of creationist astronomy.

The Bible and Astronomy, 1984 (John C. Whitcomb, BMH Books, Winona Lake, IN 46590). An excellent introduction to the subject, especially theological truth.

Creation magazine (Answers in Genesis, P.O. Box 6330, Florence, KY 41022). This quarterly magazine takes a clear and colorful look at Bible-science topics. Answers in Genesis also publishes an *Answers Update* leaflet and the *Technical Journal.*

Creation Perspective magazine (Bible-Science Association, P.O. Box 260, Zimmerman, MN 55398–0260).

Creation Research Society Quarterly (P.O. Box 8263, St. Joseph, MO 64508). Contains research articles that often touch on astronomy. This is the preeminent technical publication in creation research.

The Earth, the Stars and the Bible, 1979 (Paul B. Steidl, Presbyterian and Reformed Pub. Co., Phillipsburg, NJ 08865). A pioneer effort to interpret astronomy in terms of Scripture.

The Moon—Its Creation, Form, and Significance, 1978 (J. C. Whitcomb and Don DeYoung, BMH Books, Winona Lake, IN 46590). An analysis of the Apollo moon missions in the light of Scripture.

Reason and Revelation magazine (Apologetics Press, 230 Landmark Drive, Montgomery, AL 36117). A monthly publication with excellent articles.

Starlight and Time, 1994 (Russell Humphreys, Master Books, P.O. Box 727, Green Forest, AR 72638). This book summarizes relativistic cosmology from a creation perspective.

Internet Resources

http://seds.lpl.arizona.edu/billa/twn/top.html
Many current astronomy photos available with explanations.

**http://directory.netscape.com/reference/
education/subjects/space_exploration/nasa/**
This is a vast listing of NASA links to explore. An interesting "Astronomy Picture of the Day" is posted.

http://www.seds.org
A very clear site with current information on planets, moons, and other links.

http://antwrp.gsfc.nasa.gov
Astronomy photos.

http://geocities.com/heartland/fields/8616/
Information on how families can get started with the hobby of astronomy.

Glossary

anthropic principle The conclusion that the universe appears to be designed for the survival and well-being of mankind.

antimatter Matter with physical properties opposite that of ordinary matter. The positron, with a positive electrical charge, is the antimatter analog of the negative electron. When matter and antimatter particles meet, they annihilate each other and energy is released.

aphelion The point in a solar orbit where the object is most distant from the sun.

asteroid An object, much smaller than a planet, that orbits the sun. Many lie between the orbits of Mars and Jupiter.

astrology A nonscientific, cultic system that uses star and planet positions to explain and predict human actions.

astronomical unit The average distance between the earth and sun, 93 million miles.

astronomy The science dealing with the universe and its parts.

aurora Glowing lights in the sky, resulting from solar radiation that interacts with the earth's atmosphere. Includes the northern and southern lights, *aurora borealis* and *aurora australis.*

big bang An origin theory that asserts the universe began explosively, long ago, from a single point.

binary system Two stars orbiting each other, held together by their mutual gravity attraction.

black hole A star that has completely collapsed to a pointlike size under its own gravity.

comet A mountain-sized chunk of frozen matter that orbits the sun. Its motion alternately brings the comet near to the sun, then to the outer regions of the solar system. When close to the sun, the comet partially melts and develops a surrounding cloud of vapor and a tail. More than 200 different comets have been identified, and there are certainly many more.

creation The supernatural origin of life and matter, brought forth by the Word of God. The word *creation* also applies to the present-day universe.

density An object's mass divided by its volume. Density measures the heaviness of matter.

eclipse The movement of one astronomical object into the shadow of another.

element Any of the 111 different kinds of atoms, such as hydrogen, helium, and iron. Ninety-two elements are natural; the rest are artificially made and unstable.

equinox Two days each year when the sun appears to cross the equator, in mid-March and mid-September. At these times, day and night are equal lengths everywhere on earth.

evolution The natural, spontaneous origin of life, and its development over time. Also includes the big bang theory and stellar evolution.

galaxy A large group of stars, gas, and dust gravitationally tied together. The earth lies within the Milky Way, a spiral-shaped galaxy containing about 100 billion stars.

geocentric Centered on the earth.

gravity A fundamental force of nature that causes an attraction between all objects. The moon is held captive in its orbit by the earth's gravity.

heliocentric Centered on the sun.

light-year The distance that light travels during an entire year if unobstructed. This distance is about 6 trillion miles.

mass A measure of the total amount of matter in an object.

meteor A streak of light produced when a rock from space, usually palm-sized or smaller, passes through the earth's atmosphere and burns. These transient objects are often called "shooting stars."

Milky Way *See* galaxy.

moon Any natural object that revolves around a planet.

nebula A vast cloud of gas and dust located in space. Plural is nebulae.

neutron star *See* pulsar.

nova A star that suddenly becomes unstable and increases in brightness.

planet A large object (usually greater than 1000 miles in diameter) that circles a star. Nine known planets orbit the sun. They have no light of their own but reflect the sunlight.

pulsar A rapidly rotating, dense star. It appears to blink on and off with pulses of light radiation. Also called a neutron star.

orbit The path of the moon as it circles the earth, or the path of the earth around the sun. The shape of such orbits are ellipses.

quasar Bright starlike objects that are thought to lie at great distances. Quasar stands for quasi-stellar.

red giant A large star with a relatively cool surface temperature that gives it a red or pink appearance. Many red giant stars are about 10 to 100 times larger than the sun.

redshift A lengthening of the wavelength of light. It arises when a light source experiences strong gravity or when it is moving away from the observer. Also called Doppler shift.

revolution Orbital motion of one object around another. The earth revolves around the sun once each year.

rotation The spinning of an object about its own axis. The earth rotates once each 24 hours.

satellite A natural or man-made object that orbits a larger object. The space shuttle and the moon are satellites of the earth. In turn, the earth is a satellite of the sun.

shooting star *See* meteor.

solar system The sun and the surrounding group of objects that orbit the sun, including planets, asteroids, and comets.

supernova The explosive destruction of a massive star. The event is triggered by the collapse of the star when its nuclear fuel is exhausted.

star A sphere of gas that averages nearly a million miles in diameter, and emits vast amounts of energy. Its internal temperature is millions of degrees. The sun is an average-sized star.

sun *See* star.

tectonics Disturbance of the earth's solid crust, including continental drift and earthquake motion.

velocity A measure of the speed and direction of an object. Velocity is the distance traveled by an object in a certain time period, divided by the time elapsed.

wavelength The distance between wavecrests for any type of wave, whether water, sound, or light waves.

white dwarf A small, dense, hot type of star. Dwarf stars are about 100 times smaller than the sun.

Scripture Index

Note: References are to question numbers rather than page numbers.

171

Subject Index

Note: References are to question numbers rather than page numbers.

175

Don DeYoung holds a Ph.D. in physics from Iowa State University and a Master of Divinity from Grace Seminary. He has taught physics and astronomy since 1972 at Grace College, Winona Lake, Indiana. He has also taught and done research in California and in the South Pacific. One particular interest is sky observing, including the stars of the Southern Hemisphere. Don has written eight books on the topics of astronomy, physical science, and experimental object lessons. He firmly holds to the literal creation view of origins.